Dreams of Bill

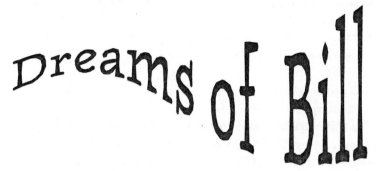

Dreams of Bill

A Collection of Funny,

Strange, and Downright Peculiar

Dreams About Our President, Bill Clinton

Edited by

Julia Anderson-Miller

and

Bruce Joshua Miller

A CITADEL PRESS BOOK
PUBLISHED BY CAROL PUBLISHING GROUP

A Citadel Press Book
Published by Carol Publishing Group
Citadel Press is a registered trademark of Carol Communications, Inc.
Editorial Offices: 600 Madison Avenue, New York, N.Y. 10022
Sales and Distribution Offices: 120 Enterprise Avenue, Secaucus, N.J. 07094
In Canada: Canadian Manda Group, P.O. Box 920, Station U, Toronto,
  Ontario M8Z 5P9
Queries regarding rights and permissions should be addressed to Carol
Publishing Group, 600 Madison Avenue, New York, N.Y. 10022

Carol Publishing Group books are available at special discounts for bulk pur-
chases, for sales promotions, fund raising, or educational purposes. Special
editions can be created to specifications. For details, contact Special Sales
Department, Carol Publishing Group, 120 Enterprise Avenue, Secaucus,
N.J. 07094

Design by Jessica Shatan

Manufactured in the United States of America
10 9 8 7 6 5 4 3 2 1

Library of Congress Cataloging-in-Publication Data

Dreams of Bill: a collection of funny, strange, and downright
      peculiar dreams about our president, Bill Clinton / edited by Julia
      Anderson-Miller, Bruce Joshua Miller.
          p.   cm.
        "A Citadel Press book."
        ISBN 0–8065–1495–7
        1. Clinton, Bill, 1946-   —Humor. I. Anderson-Miller, Julia.
      II. Miller, Bruce Joshua.
      E886.2.D74   1994
      973.929'092—dc20

Contents

Contents

Acknowledgments

Special thanks to Mary and Ray Anderson, and to Anita and Jordan Miller; thanks also to the many booksellers in the Midwest who posted our dream flier, and to Paul Bennett for his help. We would also like to thank the publisher, and our editor Kevin McDonough for his thoughtful suggestions.

Authors' Foreword

or Julia and Bruce Dream of Bill
and Dream Up *Dreams of Bill*

I was at my Macintosh formatting a book about a Japanese concentration camp in the Philippines during World War II. I was feeling rather fatigued, having been bent over like a button hook for hours. Then, out of the blue, Bill Clinton walked through the door and rubbed my neck therapeutically. It was one of those dreams where I could feel the thickness of his hands and smell the fragrance of his after-shave (sea breezy). He told me to keep working. When I woke up my neck felt better and I wondered if other people had dreamed of Bill Clinton.

Julia Anderson-Miller, Art Director at a Publishing House
Age: 36
Chicago, Illinois

Although I am far removed from Eastern thought, I have always been close to the dream state. Strangers on the elevated train or bus to and from work often tell me their dreams. Friends and coworkers have frequently asked me what I thought about their dreams. I've been called a dream magnet.

As a child, I asked my mother how I could tell if I were dreaming or awake. Her advice was to pinch myself.

I had my dream of Bill the day after President Clinton was inaugurated. I couldn't forget it. The spicy after-shave, the thick hands... my neck felt better . . . someone I voted for finally won. I knew I wasn't alone. Over dinner that night I mentioned my dream, again, to my husband, Bruce. "I just know other people are having dreams about President Clinton, I know I am not alone, we are all in the same boat."

"So," Bruce said, "what do you want to do about it?"

"Run classified ads, in all major cities, starting with Minneapolis since Minnesotans do what they are told, and see what happens," I said.

"Brilliant," said Bruce.

Early in February 2, 1993 our ad appeared:

•**Have you ever dreamt of BILL CLINTON???**•

Researchers interested in your dream for possible publication. Write a detailed account of your dream with name, age, occupation, and return address to Dreams of Bill, Box 361 • 1340 West Irving Park, Chicago, Illinois 60613

Our first dreamer responded immediately.

I had never dreamt about a politician before and neither had many of my fellow dreamers. Each Bill dream had left an impression and at times helped make a decision. To vote for Mr. Clinton or not, to give him another chance, or not. Dreamers were touched that our President cared enough to appear in their dreams or upset that he troubled their sleep.

From that first classified ad in Minneapolis, to the last newspaper article in Boulder, collecting dreams has been a remarkable experience. I like to think of this collection as a time capsule of the subconscious.

Pinch yourself.

• • •

I parked my car directly across the street from the house in which I grew up. The car was alongside the curb, and, as I stood next to it, I was facing the house belonging to the people who lived across the street.

I could see one of their kids (I think his name was Bill), doing some kind of chore in the yard. It was summer. Bill Clinton emerged from the direction of my parents' house wearing a brown summer suit and tie with a collar bar. He strode across the lawn and began talking to my neighbor Bill in a familiar and paternal tone, telling him, "Don't forget to do this, don't forget to do that." I remembered that Bill had been extremely successful in some way, and I tried to remember how—was he a Rhodes scholar?

I am a publishers' representative, and I was cleaning out the backseat of my car, which was full of book galleys, catalogues, boxes, paper, junk. Bill Clinton took an interest in what I was doing. I was a little embarrassed by all the disorder, but it didn't faze him. He sort of took over and began handing me boxes and things, helping me prepare for my next selling trip.

"You know," I said, "I represent Brookings Books; I don't know if I happen to have any of their books in here, but if I do ..." He seemed mildly interested, as he looked through the piled-high material. I took out a box that held a four-color pamphlet with a caricature of Bill Clinton on it, and an old electric clock. There was a large green Dumpster just up the street, and I looked through the box on my way over to it. Bill sort of followed me there. I pulled out the pamphlet and held it up. "That really doesn't look like you," I said.

He made a face. "The press are really wise, are'nt they."

I laughed and shook my head, "Yes," I said.

He began to go on his way along the sidewalk, as it was understood he had to meet with other people. "I've got to look at this old house over here," he said.

"You know," I said, walking up to him again, "I think you're doing a great job." He looked intent and interested when I said this. "I don't know how representative my opinion is," I said, "probably not very, but just—" At this point I wanted to say keep doing what you're doing ... child immunization ... don't listen to the press ... but I couldn't articulate it. I simply clenched my fists. He was slightly amused, and maybe even pleased.

He repeated my word with an inquisitive expression, "Just?" and clenched his fists.

"Right," I said, and he went on his way.

Bruce Miller, Publishers' Representative
Age: 39
Chicago, Illinois

At first glance, the conception of this project had nothing to do with political pundits or public opinion polls. And yet, its fulfillment was a response to the televisual sound and fury of the last presidential election. We were frustrated with the sensational approach of the news, and tired of being told what we thought. The expression of our dreams refreshed our sense of possibility, and set us in search of other people who felt as we did.

When word of our project reached people who had dreamt of Bill, they were incredulous, bewildered, and anxious to tell us that they, too, had had such dreams. Many of them thanked us for "listening," or for letting them know that they were not alone. Many of the people who wrote to us said they, like Julia, had never dreamt of a politician or celebrity before, or had rarely done so. A few of them were even having dreams about Bill Clinton every week, but didn't know why. Almost all of them said their dreams left an indelible impression. "The dream was so real," they would say, or "vivid," that they thought it might actually have happened, or might come true. An impressive number of people said they awoke with a "pounding" heart, or greatly moved and near tears, or laughing.

The word "dream" is used so often in our consumer culture to refer to common fantasies of wealth and power, one might suppose it easy to forget that the same word refers to narratives with more nourishing roots. I've learned from working on this book that people value their dreams greatly . A lot of people keep dream journals, or discuss their dreams in groups.

The provinces of sleep may be the last truly private territory left to us.

Ironically, this book adds dreams to the public media display, but, as funny and poetic as they are, they may in a very small way console us against some of the more dismal aspects of life in these times.

To read a hopeful dream can perhaps make us hopeful, as long as the dream itself is recognized as a fragmentary fiction, a collection of feelings, incidents, and memories, and not a substitute for life, action, or attempts to understand in a rational way what is going on around us. Dreams are no branch of government, and yet they should not be ignored. The political dimension is what makes this book worth reading.

I should point out that many dreamers volunteered the information that they did or did not vote for Bill Clinton. Whatever the reasons for this widespread phenomenon (people dreaming of Bill), it transcends party affiliation. This shouldn't surprise us: Clouds know no borders, and this is a book of demos, not the Democratic Party.

We feel privileged to have been the conduit for the collected writings of these dreamers. Many of them write well, and who knows but that some of them will go on to write something more. In keeping with the inclusive spirtit of this project, we have done our best to preserve the voice of each contributor, and not to tamper unnecessarily with their prose.

Dreams of Bill

A Kiss Is But a Kiss

I dreamed candidate Bill Clinton was visiting our area, and I was responsible for driving him to his quarters (a large private house) for the night. We were having a warm and friendly conversation as I pulled the car up in a circular gravel drive. We got out of the car and walked to the door of the house, where a night-light shone.

I said, "I've never kissed a candidate before. Would you mind if I kissed you?" I was aware that this was terribly bold, but I was much taken with him.

He threw back his head and laughed, saying, "Not at all!" And he embraced me in a great, warm bear-hug and kissed me on the mouth—a long, soul-melting kiss that was *delightful*. (It was a kiss so satisfying and real that I remembered every detail and feel of it on awakening.) We both laughed and went into the house, where I introduced him to a crowd of people in a wide foyer.

It turned out I was also staying there, so I soon went to my room, undressed, got into bed, and began reading with the lights on. Bill sort of wandered in wearing only his shorts and said there didn't seem to be any bed for him and could he share mine? I said, half alarmed and half sexily, "Well, why not?" He got in and we worked the *New York Times* crossword puzzle!

Then my son walked in carrying his baseball mitt and a ball. (My son was not his present age, but about ten, his age when he followed the election of JFK with great interest and wrote Kennedy a letter congratulating him on becoming President.) He said he wanted to meet Bill, too. The obliging Bill hopped out of bed and played catch and did high fives with him.

J.D.W. (Female), Retired Advertising Executive
Age: 69
Boulder, Colorado

I *kissed* Bill. Not in a sexual way really, but with more affection than lust (although I do find him attractive). I was excited about our contact and also felt a strong connection.

Allyson C. Hitt, Cartographer
Age: 24
Berkeley, California

I was at a party mingling with the other guests. Suddenly, Bill Clinton came over to me to chat. I was not surprised that he was there—it seemed natural. I was very attracted to him (as I am in reality) and I knew he felt the same toward me. As we talked he leaned over and kissed me. I'd describe "the kiss" as somewhere between friendly and passionate. By the way, he was good!! At that point, a smiling Hillary walked over to us to say hello.

I knew she had seen our "brief encounter," but I also knew that she did not mind. We all knew that our relationship would go no further.

Judy Eisenberg, Secretary
Age: 51
New York, New York

I had purchased several packages of meat the previous day, but apparently never put them in the refrigerator. I was upset to find the meat in a desk drawer, but I wanted to cook it anyway. Unsure how best to proceed, I went to Little Rock to discuss it with Bill and Hillary. I was driving down a street that looked right out of the *Andy Griffith Show*, and there was Bill sitting on the front porch and Hillary on the hood of a car. She said just to kiss her and to call her Hillary. Bill was very informal as well. They were quite congenial, but the meat issue was never resolved. . . .

J. Michael Young, Foreign Exchange Worker
Age: 25
Parsippany, New Jersey

How we met I don't know, but he came and picked me up in a limousine and I made sure that I dressed in my most feminine clothes (which I normally don't go out of my way to do). I don't remember Hillary being in existence—he was single and we were dating! I was worried about the age difference—I'm only twenty-nine and have never been involved politically, so we weren't exactly a match. Socially we were relatively incompatible. I was smitten. He was quite a gentleman and seemed to truly care for me. He was also very kind to other people.

He took me out to dinner one night. I remember he always wore a suit, and afterwards he ended up on my couch. He had loosened his tie and had no jacket on. I had kicked off my shoes and had my legs tucked under me. He leaned over, taking my face in his hands, and kissed me ever so gently. It all seemed so innocent. He was respectful even when I asked him how our relationship would ever work. (People wouldn't approve, and we would be constantly sneaking around.) We never had a more physical relationship than just kissing. We had spent a lot of time together. We were very comfortable with one another.

I awoke thinking, "Wow, I don't even think the guy is cute!"

Judy Kasner, Talent Agent
Age: 29
Chicago, Illinois

In my dream, I was having an affair with Bill. It consisted physically of no more than kissing, but he was a *good* kisser. We kept slipping away from his public appearances to go off in some corner and smooch, but the affair (and my dream) ended when the Secret Service came to visit me and warned me to stay away from Bill, saying that I would hurt his image.

S.G. (Female), Management Consultant
Age: 27
Downers Grove, Illinois

Bill has purchased a pale green house which he will put on wheels and tour the country campaigning. I thought about how it would fit in the road. Anyway, Bill was showing Hillary that the water and the air conditioner worked. I proceeded to see if there was enough space for everyone in the house. In one room, there was a group of servants sitting on the floor and on a bed watching television. In the back of the house, I started to show Bill some history books. He then kissed me. I was turned on but said, "You shouldn't be doing this." He bent his head over, then back up, and smoothed his slick hair back and said, "You're right, you're right."

Judy Golden, Operations Research Analyst
for Internal Revenue Service
Age: 26
Crownsville, Maryland

The setting was on the grounds of the White House. A group of reporters had gathered prior to a press conference. Mr. Clinton was already in attendance, but the conference had not yet started. He was squatting down, chatting with those close by. I came up to the group, and when I spotted the President, I rushed up to him. He immediately stood up and Secret Service agents came forth as though to charge me. Bewildered, I explained that I meant no harm and only wanted to give the President a little kiss, and I motioned for him to bend down. He did so, and I kissed him on the cheek. I then asked him about his neckties, whether they were chosen by him or Hillary, because he seemed to wear a lot with polka dots. He told me he chooses his own neckties. I told him that I just love dots, and he smiled and replied, "So do I!"

Marjorie Beard, Housewife
Age: 64
Arnold, Missouri

I was sitting in a restaurant, eating dinner with Bill. I was laughing and we were talking about the baseball game we just came from. We started kissing at the table, and everyone was looking at us.

Bill said to me, "Let's go somewhere more private."

I agreed.

He opened the door to a limo. I was sitting in the limo, wondering what my husband would think. Bill told me not to worry—"It's just us."

Next thing I know, we're in bed together, and let me say it was *great.* He was the best love maker in the world. He kissed so *good.*

Tammy Anderson, Housewife
Age: 25
St. Louis, Missouri

A Vote of Encouragement

I was primping and preening myself, because I knew I was going to see the President. As a surrogate mother for the Clintons, I had just given birth to their child. The President walked up to me and said, "Mrs. Peterson, you're looking very fit after the pregnancy."

When I woke up I felt slim, beautiful, and concluded that the President is a smart man! In real life I am a mother of two girls and have never been a surrogate parent.

Lydia Barden Peterson, Special Needs Teacher
Age: 36
Maplewood, Minnesota

A warmly lit corridor contained no one else but the esteemed President Clinton. He was wearing a well-fitting suit and was stooped down looking directly at me as I approached him. There, as I stood before him, he extended his arm to shake my hand. It was very comforting. Our grips were firm but understanding, and most of all extremely affirming. At this he arose to say, "You're doing a fine job, don't give up. I didn't."

It was a time in the semester when I was under much academic stress, and subconsciously wished for an escape. After the dream, I was aware of the new day before me, and aware that there was no fear within me any longer. I no longer felt any anxiety. Instead I felt completely assured and confident. As I sat to take the exam that once so frightened me, I was reassured by the mental images left with me from the dream. Thanks for the "A," Mr. President!

André Robert Rabalais, College Student, Junior Level
Age: 20
Bossier City, Louisiana

My most memorable "dream of Bill" took place in a department store where I was working as the special events manager. Bill was making a special appearance in conjunction with a "Made in the USA" promotion we were doing, which drew crowds in the thousands. I just remember standing in the crowd, in between racks of clothes, applauding the President's speech, when he looked right at me, smiled, and gave me the thumbs-up sign.

Afterwards, when the crowd had dispersed, I had the opportunity to meet Bill personally. He told me he was really impressed with my work in pulling such a successful event together, and then asked if I would be interested in joining his staff. The next thing I knew, I was in Washington working side-by-side with Bill—as a newly elected senator!

Jill M. Fiore, Assistant Director for Public Relations
Age: 26
Pittsburgh, Pennsylvania

I was in a government office building (I work for the government). President Clinton came down the hall alone, in a suit and tie, shook our hands, and said, "Keep trying. Do not give up. Do the right thing no matter what."

Jenith Stodolski, Engineering Technician
Age: 54
Durango, Colorado

I recently got my diploma (G.E.D.), and I dreamed that when I went to pick up my diploma, Bill told me to never stop learning, and I awoke because I had to go to the bathroom.

Margaret A. Gary, Mother/Business Student
Age: 27
Pittsburgh, Pennsylvania

In the first part of the dream (vaguely remembered), an older, more conservative woman friend of mine was criticizing Clinton. In the next part, Clinton and I were lying on our backs on a mattress or low bed with blankets. As a concerned friend (with no undertones of romance or eroticism), I cradled Clinton's head on my left shoulder and comforted him, telling him to stick to his goals and principles and not let negative criticism get him down.

Vicki Bruns Briggs, Artist/Library Clerk
Age: 49
Champaign, Illinois

During the period between the election and the inauguration, Bill Clinton was staying with my family and me in my home in Oregon. In the daytime, he would go off and deal with the business of Washington, with all the gossip and criticism of the press and politicians there, and come home exhausted and almost comatose sitting on the end of the sofa. He liked being around the family clatter, but had no energy left to engage with others, and we tried to be sensitive to this. I went over to him at one point to say, "Don't let the critics get you down. There'll always be complaints no matter what tack you take. Just do what you believe in." Even without looking up, he seemed to have heard what I said.

Marnie Glaser, School Psychologist
Age: 43
Chicago, Illinois

Bill Clinton and I were having a meeting. We were sitting (half sitting and half lying) fully clothed on a double bed, and I was giving him advice on being President. I do not remember all that we were talking about, except that I told him he had to be more of a cheerleader about himself. I remember the room looked like a quaint bed-and-breakfast, with a table near the windows. Also, there were other people (strangers) milling about. I have to say that I felt very moved by the dream when I woke up, and really felt like I had been with the President.

Barbara H. Haacke, Homemaker
Age: 40
Darien, Connecticut

All's Well That Ends Well

My husband and I were standing in a reception line, waiting to meet Bill Clinton. Suddenly he was standing beside us, shaking my husband's hand vigorously and smiling as if we were old friends. "I know about the wonderful work you're doing in the arts," he said to my husband, who runs a financially beleaguered arts organization. "We just have to get through November 2nd, then I'll see to it that you have more money to work with."

He patted my husband on the back and extended his hand to me. "And by the way," he said, sliding his left hand down into his suit pocket, "Happy Birthday." He produced a beautiful bracelet, a delicate and unusual design of pale green peridots—my birthstone. It was, in fact, a week or so before my real birthday. "I've gotta run," he said and disappeared, leaving my husband and me waving happily into space.

Deborah Galyan, Writer/Editor
Age: 37
Lake Forest, Illinois

I was shopping at the St. Louis Galleria with Bill. (In real life I'm sure I wouldn't refer to him by his first name, but in the dream he was just "Bill"!) He was dressed very casually, and we were talking about small, insignificant things. We went into stores like The Gap and Banana Republic. While we were in one of the stores, Bill picked out a nice shirt to try on. He disappeared into the dressing room and then reappeared wearing the new shirt. He left his old one in the dressing room. Then, to my horror, he said, "I'm ready to get out of here. Let's go." I tried to appear nonchalant, although I was disgusted because he didn't pay for the shirt. We left and went to get some café mocha at the St. Louis Bread Company. Meanwhile, a couple of embarrassed Secret Service men slipped away and returned to the clothing store to pay for Bill's shirt.

My husband enjoyed repeating this dream to all his conservative Republican coworkers. They like to tease me because my views are pretty liberal, and I voted for Clinton.

Shana Durham, Advertising and Marketing Consultant
Age: 23
Richmond Heights, Missouri

My brother from Washington and I were on a plane—I guess he was the pilot. We kept going along the ground for some time. Then up into the sky we sailed—just making it—above the trees and buildings. Up above the clouds we did go, stopping at a space station in the sky. My brother and a strange man walked ahead of me. The stranger was a lot taller than my brother! They both wore dark suits and were walking slowly into a room where the plane was being monitored on a TV. Quite a few people were standing around. I didn't get into the room myself, but I could see what was going on.

As the two men appeared at the doorway, the stranger turned—it was President Clinton! He waved and smiled at me, as if it say, "Everything is going to be all right!" Then I woke up!

E.A.L.T. (Female), Retired Babysitter
Age: 60
Pelican Rapids, Minnesota

Bill Clinton is summoning hippie guys and gals from many communes around the country to help run the government. I remember thinking that's a little radical and wondering how the general public will react, but I also think that it is pretty wise and cool. I watch as six guys from one commune are piling rowboats that are dirty from traveling across the waterways to get to Washington.

Later, Bill and I are leading government groups, and we realize that we are having too many meetings and processing too much, that people are frustrated and not working well together. We decide to have no more meetings, to just relax and allow things to work out more naturally. (I remember a little concern about how we will deal with conflict when it comes up, but also realize that with a more relaxed atmosphere, fewer conflicts would arise.)

Bill Wing, Psychotherapist
Age: 39
St. Louis, Missouri

Armageddon had become a reality! Bill Clinton was President. When Armageddon happened, it took everyone by surprise, because it was so quick, so sudden! Needless to say, I was panicked, as were billions of other people!

There were terrible things going on, very similar to Revelations; however, with a more high-technology twist!

It was broadcast that Clinton, his family, and the cabinet members were airborne in a doomsday plane, that could stay aloft for thirty days. But President Clinton's team was considering certain secret bunkers to go to—and inform the nation what to do!

It was horrifying to see the Beast standing in the temple and the Antichrist threatening the world! Bill suddenly approached the Antichrist from out of nowhere and challenged him in many physical feats—like a decathlon athlete. The Antichrist was winning, then the Beast started to attack Bill, but he defeated the Beast . . . when Jesus came in and defeated the Antichrist and then in an earth-shaking groan from the earth, Heaven appeared with God and all of his angels. There was *Bill* smiling and shaking hands with angels and Jesus. Wow, what a moment in time!

David Singleton, Certified Nurse's Aide
Age: 39
Boulder, Colorado

Auditoriums and Stages

Bill was hosting *Late Night With David Letterman.* As I was watching the show it struck me that there was something wrong with Bill's eyes. He was blind, but he had been putting on a good act pretending he was not blind. He went on making good jokes, and the audience laughed and laughed. Meanwhile, the television camera zoomed in on his eyes, which were white and blind.

Next, Bill put on a woman's dress and began to dance all over the set. Two men danced with him (two security guards or bodyguards). I was, all of a sudden, a stagehand. I was no longer viewing the scene from my home, but was actually participating in the dance. I noticed that Bill had become sexually aroused due to the fact that he was wearing a woman's dress. The audience noticed this as well. I was very embarrassed for him, but he didn't seem to care. Instead of running off the set, he played it out and continued the show.

> W.A.S. (Female), Recent College Grad
> Looking for Work as an Illustrator
> Age: 24
> Waterbury, Connecticut

J ust after the election of Bill Clinton, I dreamed that he asked to see me. I went to a theater and there onstage, alone, sitting on a Victorian sofa, bright yellow with a floral pattern, was Bill Clinton. I sat beside him, and he assured me that everything would be okay, and he understood how I felt about things. The only other thing I recall was that there were bright lights shining on us, and on Bill's face, and his smile was glowing and his cheeks were rosy.

W.B.K. (Male), Writer
Age: 37
Reynoldsburg, Ohio

I was a somewhat nervous and confused campaign worker who had basic research duties on the Clinton-Gore bus tour. Actually, closer to an administrative assistant who pushed paper and sent faxes. The staff I worked for traveled together and set up camp before Bill, Al, Hillary, and Tipper would arrive. I think we were south. I think maybe Louisiana. . . .

Anyway, it was a normal, chaotic workday of paper-cup coffee, temporary help, phones and faxes in constant ringing and motion, people yelling, and the press. Al Gore arrives without the parade and starts talking to a more important group in our camp—people I suppose I should know, like, they would have been my bosses. . . . However, this was one of those dreams where I was kind of a fish out of water with people I have never known (I've never had an administrative job).

Al and the group are worried, and they're looking around and talking, and I'm watching them looking around and talking.

Finally, they walk over to me, seemingly at random, and a man and a woman professional are now standing next to George Stephanopoulos, who is massaging his throat while Al Gore just stands behind them looking at me, his usual stiff-as-a-board self.

The man and woman professional explain to me that George won't be able to introduce the future team at a huge rally that is getting louder down the hall. George, it is explained, has "Bill's sore throat"—and that *I'll* have to introduce them. (There is also a lot of screaming about the room, at sound technicians about how they'll have to increase the volume for Bill as well, for this was apparently the final days, where he lost his voice.) The volume would have to be super loud, but everybody was also worried about the microphone's feedback.

Anyway, within moments, I'm being whisked down a hall, just as Bill and Hillary arrive . . . and there's a lot of backstage hysteria . . . and soon I'm at the curtain, while an equally nervous soundman hands me a hot-feedback mike, and I'm asking staff superiors what exactly I'm supposed to say . . . and they tell me frantically and all at once to just introduce them as the next White House team.

Before going out onstage, Al Gore gives me a light tap and a stiff wink that everything is fine . . . and in seconds, with loud, reverberating feedback, I'm on stage with blaring stage lights, realizing just how incredibly enormous this crowd is. . . . A few murmurs and whistles can be heard, but mostly everybody is wincing from the feedback. I look back, and for the first time I really see Bill, standing calmly, waiting to be introduced at stage right, hands folded over documents.

And nervous, but elated and proud, I "go for broke," that is, I scream with all the energy of the Democratic Convention: "Ladies and Gentlemen, the next President of the United States . . . . Bill Clinton!"

Feedback aside, everything's in sync now.

And the place is up for grabs as I hand him the microphone, clapping just as enthusiastically as the rest of what seems like thousands. I slip backstage, overwhelmed by an explosion of welcoming applause by this massive audience.

The electricity, and the enormity of power found with the rally's thunderous applause toward this calm man, resonated into my waking state.

Dennis Frank, Filmmaker
Age: 33
Chicago, Illinois

I dreamt that Bill Clinton was touring the country, promoting his economic plan. He was seated on a stage with the other participants, in a half-circle, in plain school-type chairs, with overhead stage lights. It was in an auditorium, I think at a local public school. There were about eight or so participants, and Bill was seated just left of center.

In the dream, I was some kind of coordinator or helper in this forum. I was kneeling onstage, behind the participants. I whispered over to Bill. He was about ten feet away. I asked if there was anything I could get for him. With a warm smile, he leaned backward and to his right toward me, held up a can of orange soda, gestured the can toward me, and said, "No thanks, I'm okay."

The dream was so vivid that I've started drinking different brands of orange and diet orange soda. In part, it's a weird way of feeling a sense of solidarity with the President. And, I'm trying to identify the brand he had in the dream. I think it must be an East Coast brand, perhaps Hoffman's or White Rock. I think I'd recognize the brand if I saw it. So I keep looking.

Sam Hochberg, Attorney
Age: 43
Portland, Oregon

In my dream, I can remember meeting Bill and he was so friendly. Then a lot of time passed, and I ran into him again and he said, "Hi, Janeen!" I was so surprised and excited that he remembered my name! During this second part of the dream, he was trying to be a "really cool" President and was hosting *Saturday Night Live* and wearing jeans, a black leather vest, and no shirt. Can you imagine?

Janeen Rubino, Administrative Assistant/Graduate Student
Age: 29
Pleasanton, California

I was sitting on the floor in front of a stage. There were other people sitting on the floor but no one sitting to my right. Bill Clinton stood on stage performing Steve Martin's first play. He was playing Picasso for the most part and drifted in and out of other roles. At one point during the performance he stepped off stage and sat next to me on the floor. Everyone was very quiet waiting to see what he would say. He said nothing, however. He just sat there looking straight ahead. Then, without looking, he picked up my right hand with his left hand and held it on his knee for about a minute. My heart pounded thinking that I was going to have to enter into this improvisation by saying something witty. Nothing happened though. Bill got up and continued his performance in the play. At the climax of the show the lead woman said, "Bill, don't you remember me? We grew up in the same town. We did tons of stuff together!" He turned to her and said, "That may be true. But, the things that stay in my mind are the things that have touched my heart." My right hand was on fire. Then I woke up.

Elizabeth Ferguson
Age: NA
Evanston, Illinois

At a performance of Shakespeare put to music, I'm looking at chamber groups and period instruments set up willy-nilly throughout the concert hall. A woman, a fellow student and singer, drags a cart with her. Next thing I know, we're under fire. We're coming out of the woods into a field. Beside me is Bill Clinton in a helmet. I'm trying to assess whether he's a good leader under the circumstances. A plane dropping bombs hits and blows up the boyfriend of the other singer. In the field, we're seated at tables ready to order from a menu. The singer orders an enormous steak meal. I look at those with me, wondering how anyone whose boyfriend's just been blown up would have the appetite.

Joan Fisher, Sleep Recorder-Interpreter for Hospitals/Poet
Age: NA
Evanston, Illinois

I saw two people sparring in the arena below. Bill Clinton and my mom were with me in the stands. I turned to Bill Clinton with disgust. I said, "I'll be on the Peace Committee." He nodded and smiled. In the dream, President Bush was an enemy. My mom was an ally, although she still thought I was sorry to be gay. I told her, "Gay people aren't sorry to be gay; they're sorry that there are bigots in society!"

Sandy Kuntz, Educator
Age: 27
San Diego, California

I was sitting by myself at a long lunch table in a large auditorium much like the centers set up for flood victims. Willard Scott, the weather guy, and President Clinton sat down across from me. Scott was on the left, Clinton the right. I proceeded to tell Scott and President Clinton why they should go to southeast Kansas to see Big Brutus, which is a gigantic machine/scoop shovel that used to scrape up coal in that area many years ago. It is now a tourist attraction, can be toured, and is something that should *not* be missed. I think I persuaded Willard to go see it, but President Clinton listened, then got up and left without a word to me.

Dawn Vohsen, Journal Editing Coordinator
Age: 41
Maryland Heights, Missouri

There were tables set up in a large room which seemed like a high school gymnasium. I was seated at a card table which was to the left of a larger table. It seemed as if it were Election Day, or something.

As I was sitting there, looking at notes I had written in pencil on a tiny yellow Post-It memo pad, President Clinton strode in and took the seat to my immediate right. I looked up from my note pad and said, "Hello, Mister President." He replied with a good-natured joke (I can't remember what), addressing me by my first name. I then picked up a book I had been reading and continued to read, as if it were no big deal to be seated next to the President. At that point, I woke up.

> J.H.S. (Male), Unemployed Vietnam-Era Veteran
> Age: 51
> Schuylkill Haven, Pennsylvania

President Clinton was on stage in a school auditorium, giving a speech. His head and trunk and arms were perfectly still. His legs, however, were clogging.*

('Executing a dance in which the performer wears clogs and beats out a clattering rhythm upon the floor.)

> Jill Draper, Full-time Mom
> Age: 36
> University City, Missouri

It was World Youth Day in Denver.

People as far as you could see—noisy, confusion.

Suddenly silence. Everyone silent and surprised—eyes turn to stage—President Bill Clinton and Pope John Paul II are signing in American sign language.

B.F.G. (Male), Retired Federal Employee
Age: 76
Denver, Colorado

There is an intermission and I was backstage. As host of the show, I was surprised to suddenly hear tumultuous applause. I looked up just in time to see the very end of an interview in which Bill Clinton was interviewing Bob Dylan. As they both walked off-stage toward me, I stopped the President (whom I seemed to know well) and I said, "So, Bill, was that okay?" He said, "Yeah, it was fine, everything went just fine." I said, "So I don't need to edit it? We can broadcast the interview just as it is?" He said, "Well, actually, why don't you let me come back and we'll redo the interview sometime, because I think we could get it better." I replied, "Oh great, I'm glad you want to come back. It would be great to have you come back another time." The President smiled and said, "I'll keep coming back as long as Bob keeps buying the tickets."

Nick Forester, Musician/Radio Show Producer and Host
Age: 38
Boulder, Colorado

I am in a small, dark auditorium where beautiful gowns are being modeled. I am backstage with other models, waiting for my turn to go on. Two of the female models walk onstage and then down the runway, one at a time. Next it is my turn. Everyone claps just like they did for the previous two dresses. When I return backstage, I study my dress in an oval full-length mirror trimmed with smooth brass. The front of the dress is a simple, elegant design of black fabric.

I look over my shoulder into the mirror and view the back of the dress . . . zigzags of multicolored sequins . . . red at the waist . . . gold, blue-green, and black. I love it. The back side of the dress is gorgeous! I am fascinated that from one perspective the front of the dress looks traditional, plain, and simple—and that from the back it is colorful, unpredictable, and complex.

Suddenly, I find myself in an average four- or five-bedroom house, one story high. The house is clean, looks lived-in, and has interesting items in it. The colors are cornflower blue with white, and the style of the furniture is mainstream American.

It is early in the morning. I wonder, "Why am I at someone's home so early? Hmmmmmm. Oh, well—no wonder. I live here. Well then, who am I living with?" In walks President Clinton, who is returning from a morning walk for an important meeting. "Oh, yes," I realize, "I'm living with President Clinton at his house now."

I recall how in a previous dream Governor Jerry Brown (then a candidate for Democratic nominee for President) visited my house. In this dream when I am with Clinton, I'm at his house.

Bill Clinton looks handsome. As he walks past me, he stops, looks directly at me, eye to eye, but only briefly, and acknowledges my presence. We do not speak; however, I realize that he will be listening to the important men in suits who are coming through the front door now for a meeting. They look like advisers. I tell myself that this is showing me how I will feel during his administration. He is half interested in me, I do have access to him and he is perceptive and direct, but he is on a tight schedule and surrounded by the powerful retinue of political advisers who have more of his time than us regular folks.

I decide to hang out at Clinton's house a while longer while he is at the meeting. The men are served orange juice. We talk. The atmosphere is productive and relaxed.

Then I hear music from another room. I wonder if I will get to hear Bill Clinton play his saxophone.

Jill Gregory, Director of a Center for Dreams
Age: NA
Navato, California

Bill and Al

I dreamt Bill Clinton and Al Gore were walking down a parade route in Washington to make a speech in front of the White House. I dreamt they were both shot by someone en route, but they kept on walking. Each was shot once—Clinton in the side, and Gore in the stomach. As they got to where the speech was to be made, Gore fell on the ground in pain and curled up in a fetal position, but Clinton went up and made his speech, no problem. Gore then turned into a woman.

Later on, I'm in the White House—just a spectator, an observer, soaking up the experience. I have a guitar in my hands and unconsciously plunk a few chords. This changes the formal mood, and some guy comes up and wants to hear music! So, he turns on a jukebox and disrupts the proceedings. Things start to get out of hand at this point—some little girl unleashes a blood-curdling scream (just to let off a little steam and get some attention)—there's more gunplay, and a fight in the corner—I even have a sexual encounter—significant only because this all happens in the White House.

Tony Garry, Self-employed Musician
Age: 41
St. Paul, Minnesota

In this dream, Bill sensed that I was at a public pool, but there were few people in the pool. The pool was, I think, an outdoor pool, but there was an unexposed air.

I noticed that Bill Clinton was swimming about with Al Gore.

It seemed as if they were acting and trying to be younger than they were.

I stepped out of the pool, and I noticed that they did too. They had big smiles on their faces, but they looked fake.

I looked at them and they at me. My expression was not pleasant toward them but not altogether bitter. Al Gore's smile vanished and he gave me a not-so-pleasant look in return.

Bill Clinton did a backward dive into the water, but it was all an act to impress me and it was fake.

When I woke up I wondered why I felt so . . . almost disgusted by Bill. The dream was a little hard for me to accept because I took Bill to be the best candidate. My mind hadn't changed but it gave me a different opinion about Bill Clinton.

Zachary Santamaria, Student
Age: 16
New York, New York

I had just completed my first small patchwork quilt and had just started a full-size quilt.

In my dream I was standing in a room completely surrounded by different fabrics. Fabric pieces were on the chairs, on the lamps, on the bookcases, plus a large number of small pieces scattered on the floor. I was all alone and feeling a lot of pressure—stress, confusion, and even panic.

In walked Bill Clinton and Al Gore. I don't remember their faces at all—just two males, tall, with dark hair—but I knew right away who they were. They both put a comforting arm on my shoulders—one on each side of me—and began telling me that they had done this many times before and knew what they were doing. They assured me of this a few times—and all of a sudden, out of complete chaos emerged a beautiful quilt. Peace, quietness, and a gentle, loving feeling filled the room—and me. They disappeared right after that—but I could still feel their comforting presence when I woke up.

> Maureen Wilson, Part-time Cashier
> Age: 45
> Durham, North Carolina

I am at the White House for some sort of reception. I am very happy to be there. I am in an office with the President, the Vice President, and some other officials. Everything is very friendly. We are trying to figure out where we can go camping without too much attention. We want to have an old-fashioned campout, just the Pres., the V.P., and me and maybe one or two Secret Service agents. We finally decide on someplace in the Smoky Mountains where we think we can escape the crowds. Everyone is very happy about the decision, and I am feeling very excited about the prospect until Clinton and Gore stand up to shake my hand and I see that they are only wearing boxer shorts and knee socks from the waist down.

They don't seem to realize their predicament. From the waist up, they're very formally attired in conservative suits. I try to point this out to them, but they seem oblivious. I feel I must make them aware of the situation. The rest of the dream, I am very anxious, as I cannot make them see what's going on. I feel bad for them, and also annoyed, as I know that this will somehow interfere with our camping trip.

Gary Culver, Hypnotherapist
Age: 40
Kaneohe, Hawaii

My old girlfriend from high school days and I were discussing politics in a posh hotel bar. In walked Bill Clinton and Al Gore. They overheard our spirited discussion and sat down beside us. They asked us to join them in their hotel suite to finish our discussion.

After finishing our cocktails, my friend and I proceeded to the room number that Bill and Al gave us. We knocked and heard someone say "Come in." As we entered we were surprised to see the future President and V.P. sitting there with only their jogging shorts on. I went over to sit next to Bill Clinton and was surprised to see all kinds of red and blue tattoos all over his body. I said, "Bill, why do you have all these red and blue tattoos on your body?"

He said, "Joan, red and blue tattoos and white skin—red, white, and blue—I am an all-American boy!" I laughed and my dream ended there.

Joan McCormick, Homemaker
Age: 52
Troy, Michigan

Bill Clinton and Al Gore were going through a huge crowd, shaking hands with everyone and smiling. I was super excited when Bill came and shook my hand and looked into my eyes. I wanted to get in my two cents worth like everyone else, and I asked, "Why does the U.S. allow nuclear facilities and materials to be on major earthquake fault zones? We could have our own Chernobyl caused by a major quake." He stopped walking for a moment and seemed genuinely interested and said he would get Al Gore to check on it. Al was standing there listening, too.

Then he went on shaking hands with everyone.

Donna Rahman, Housewife/Mother
Age: 39
San Jose, California

Bill Protects Me

Myself and a few of my friends (all women) were in the dining room of my home. I looked out the window and I saw a tornado a few feet from the window. I yelled to everyone, "It's a tornado! Take cover," which they did, underneath the dining room table. I did not, as I was watching the tornado approach the house. My friends began calling to me to take cover, when President Clinton said, "Dolores, please come underneath the table," and he extended his hand to me.

I did not want to take it, but he was insistent and finally I did. Just then the windows were shattered, and the President threw himself over me and my friends to protect us from the tornado. Then I woke up and felt as if I really had this experience, and I had seen the President, and he had taken my hand.

Dolores Flores, Telephone Company Employee
Age: 39
Dearborn, Michigan

I am trying to move into a new apartment, but I am sick and very down. Hillary and Bill come over to help me move. When they see how sick I am, they are very concerned. Bill puts his arm around my waist to support me. They take me to their town house (not the White House) and nurse me to health. I wake up feeling warm, cared for, and safe.

Amber Keyser, Specialist at a Psychiatric
Treatment Center for Teens
Age: 22
Wilsonville, Oregon

My dream was shortly after the election. I was in a cocktail lounge when I saw Bill. He was smiling and looking very good. I started to feel very chilly and was very glad when Bill came over and very gently placed a white sweater around my shoulders. It was a very reassuring feeling to me.

P.G. (Female), Former Librarian, Model
Age: 39
Dania, Florida

There were seven people, including Bill and myself, who were being held in a wood-paneled apartment while bombs were going off all around us. Bill and I were sitting on the sofa, and he said he would protect me. He had his arm around me and our legs were intertwined; I was on his left, his left leg was on the bottom, my right leg crossed over his left, his right leg crossed over my right, and my left leg crossed over his right, if that makes any sense.

I felt as if someone had been hugging me. All day, I walked around feeling especially wonderful.

Beth Oast, Graduate Student in a Library Science Program
Age: 28
Dartsmouth, Virginia

I was in a very large room—the impression being that the room was a part of a huge art gallery.

The walls were stucco, with beautiful Mexican tile floors. The only furniture was a white couch with big plumpy pillows and cushions, and I knew it was not for use but only display. The entrance to the room was a double wrought-iron gate opening in the middle, and the ceiling arched up into a dome, while the gates were straight across their top. In this peaceful and beautiful setting, there was the most horrible loud hard-rock music about to blast my head off, and I was considering closing the wrought-iron gates and realized at the same time there was no way they could close out the horrible cacophony coming from outside the room.

It was at this moment President Clinton came down the hall and gently closed the gates behind him as he entered the room, and the noise stopped.

He came across the room, gently took my hand, and led me to the untouchable white couch and, with a slight flourish, indicated I was to be seated. He then sat on the couch beside me and turned my shoulders to face him, and as I gazed into his eyes and looked at his smile, I was impressed with what sexy lips he had, but more importantly the overwhelming feeling of true gentleness and kindness emanating from him made me think, "This is a really nice man."

Jacquoline Cherry, Homemaker
Age: 59
Poway, California

Brother, Can You Spare a Dime

I dreamt that I was in a public park, sitting on a bench, and Bill Clinton and his daughter Chelsea came and sat right next to me. They were both wearing jeans and a white T-shirt. All I could do was sit and stare. . . . The next thing I remember is getting invited to the White House. Mr. Clinton gave me his phone number and said I was welcome anytime. . . .

Then I realized in my dream, I WAS A HOMELESS PERSON!!! Chelsea gave me ten dollars and wished me luck!!

Larissa Zakharin, Secretary for a Mortgage Company
Age: 20
Santa Monica, California

The Prez and $5.00 to Boot

Met Bill Clinton on the beach:
    Said: Where you get those
    boots, Bill?

The President answered: "Found them
in the sand."

So says I: That's stealing, Bill . . .
They belong to the County! The Prez
replies: "No they don't . . . they have
'Coast Guard' written all over them."

So yours truly asks: Bill: How
about some small change . . .
anything you got in your pocket:

And Bill reaches down deep, to
come up with a 1943 white penny
(which I promptly took to the
Coin Shoppe and received $5.00
for).

Joe Gleason, Jr., Senior Aide: Marine Education Center
and Aquarium
Age: 63
Biloxi, Mississippi

Butcher, Baker, Candlestick Maker

I woke up to look at the clock, and there was Bill holding out his hand and telling me it was time to get up and go to work. I grabbed his hand and all of a sudden we were in my car driving to the restaurant. Sometimes I was driving and sometimes he was driving. Next, we were wearing our matching chef's uniforms, baking away, when I noticed drops of blood on the floured work surface. I looked up at Bill and his palms were bleeding. He had the stigmata. He was just standing there holding out his hands, bleeding. His mouth was moving really fast, but no sound was coming out. I smelled something burning. I woke up. It was time to go to work.

Beth Lisick, Pastry Chef
Age: 24
Saratoga, California

I had two dreams about Bill Clinton that I would like to share. The first dream I had was one where Bill worked as a clerk in

Dominick's grocery store to show what a down-to-earth guy he was. He hung up my stuff and I noticed that his name tag said "Bubba."

In my second dream, Bill had an office in Park Ridge, Illinois (which is where Hillary is from). He had a framed picture of k. d. lang's album *Ingénue* on the wall. I went to see Bill because my favorite antique store in Park Ridge had gone out of business and I wanted to know why because he owned the store.

Alison Dasso, College Student
Age: 19
Buffalo Grove, Illinois

I dreamt that Clinton was a traveling salesman named Roy Butler. He was a typical fifties-style rural huckster, with a porkpie hat and plaid jacket: probably a lot like his own father, Bill Blythe. He was selling lightbulbs. These were revolutionary lightbulbs—not only energy efficient but something about the light they cast was specially illuminating. They were clear glass and had really complex filaments that you could see glowing different colors (as is often the case in dreams, I could look at the glowing filament but the light didn't hurt my eyes). These newfangled, space-age lightbulbs were a boon to mankind in some metaphysical way. So even though Butler/Clinton was a "slick" dude, there was something endearing and innocent about the product he was touting . . . and he sincerely believed in it. And he believed in it because it was the genuine article!

Nan McCulloch, Screenwriter
Age: 41
Ferndale, Michigan

The youngest of my cats, Marvel (who incidentally is black-and-white like Socks), had been seriously injured, I think by a hit-and-run driver. I had him in my arms, and I was terrified that he would bleed to death before I could get help. I was in a triangle of tall buildings—confused and kept getting lost. I felt panicked because my cat was dying. I knew that if I could only find Bill Clinton, Marvel would be all right. Much to my enormous relief, I found Bill, who was a vet. My cat survived.

> Mary Ann T. Beverly, Writer
> Age: 40
> Columbia, South Carolina

I met a man at a convention. We realized we were instantly compatible; so much so that I gave up my career to work as a secretary in his office just so we could be together. He had told me he was a successful businessman who ran a marketing company. On my first day of working with him, he said he had to go to a lunch meeting. He left the office and took an elevator to the bottom of the building. I followed him. When the elevator doors opened on the basement of this building, I realized I was at a huge convention where this "marketing businessman" was accepting the Democratic nomination for President since he was Bill Clinton. I woke up feeling stupid that I hadn't realized who he was sooner!!!

> A.B.G. (Female), Media Promotion
> Age: 30
> New Orleans, Louisiana

Bill Clinton was the referee at the final Olympic baseball game. I was on the bench, it being my duty to tote the water and towels to the "Dream Team."

During time-outs, Mr. Clinton would come over and talk to me. He was so fascinated by my conversation, he forgot about the game. As a result, the Dream Team lost the Gold Medal and everyone blamed him. I was all set to defend him when he began to tell reporters that it was all my fault.

I felt so betrayed.

Jennifer Poiry, Student/Customer Service Representative
Age: 23
Leo, Indiana

Bill was a professor of political science and I was one of his students here in Buffalo. We fell in love and had great sex. He was married to Hillary and I was single. Al Gore yelled at me and told me I was a home-wrecker!! But I didn't care because I loved Bill.

M.A.M. (Female), Mother/Part-time Insurance Secretary
Age: 28
Buffalo, New York

My three grown children appeared in my dream, and it seemed quite natural that they should look exactly as they did about thirty-five years ago. Our living room was decorated beautifully in preparation for their little guests. It must have been a birthday party, because the children arrived carrying gifts.

Suddenly, the room was filled to capacity. I became uptight because the clown I had promised had not arrived. They all started screaming, "Where's the clown!" Just when I couldn't stand it any longer, the clown, who was Bill Clinton, arrived. He cavorted all over the place, delighting the youngsters. It was in this joyful setting that I left the party and awakened.

Ruth Rupp, Housewife
Age: 71
Pittsburgh, Pennsylvania

I dreamt about Mr. Clinton just after the election. As a former priest, I am still dealing with issues surrounding the ministry. In the dream, I have been assigned to a Catholic Campus Ministry Center at the University of New Mexico. I am to be the assistant to Bill Clinton, who will be the pastor.

In the dream, "Father Clinton" is celebrating Mass at the Center and I am thinking that he will be all right as the head of the Center, but that I will have to be the inspiration to keep our ministry exciting and lively. In the dream, I perceived Clinton as efficient but somewhat conservative.

Stephen Shimek, Social Worker
Age: 54
Oak Park, Illinois

I was on line at a buffet-style restaurant—the type you find off the New Jersey Turnpike—and Bill Clinton was working the cash register. He was wearing a little paper server's hat, and the media were there, and a large crowd was gathering. I was with my parents, who were excited to meet him. I remember looking at Clinton and thinking he seemed so pleasant that I felt bad for saying negative things about him, like that he wouldn't really make any changes. I felt like an atheist in a church, as if my critical thoughts on Bill made me some kind of subversive in the House of Bill. When it was my turn to pay, and I stood in front of him and another man who was a friend of his, he says half to me, and half to his friend, "My, you are a beautiful young lady—isn't she just gorgeous!"

This friend nods with exaggerated enthusiasm. So then I start thinking, "He knows I thought badly of him, and he's trying to make me feel guilty." Then his head starts to inflate—but all his features stayed together—like a Bill Plympton (jeez!) cartoon. That was the end.

P.W. (Female), Student
Age: 22
New York, New York

Campaigns and Coverage

I was an undecided voter—Clinton or, I didn't know. I had a vivid dream where I was interviewing Bill and Hillary (I'm a former TV talk-show host!). They were really very open, engaging people who took my questions seriously and seemed to answer me very truthfully. I can't remember the exact gist of our conversation, but I know that the dream felt really very pleasant. I had a wonderful time chatting it up with the Clintons, and I found them to be the exact opposite of the Washington establishment. *Washington, D.C., is my hometown, and I lived on Capitol Hill for five years.*

Gwenn Kelly, Business Television Consultant
Age: 47
Palos Verdes, California

I dreamt I was at a rally for Bill Clinton at a local university. While strolling around trying to find my friends, who had located a good place to stand to see the action, I came upon Clinton.

I was concerned that his lack of candor about the draft situation would screw up his candidacy. We started to talk. I said, "Why didn't you come clean, tell the whole story? You're going to have to deal with it eventually, you know." He nodded and looked so sad. When I got back to my friends, they had let another person take the place they had promised to save for me. I was upset and got into conversation with some other people about Clinton and about how my friends wouldn't save the promised space. One of the people told me the reason for the crowded condition here was that because of the economy, the parking space for the university had been cut down to one small parking lot. And more cuts were yet to come.

Terry Popp, Working on Creative Writing Ph.D.
at the Union Institute
Age: 64
Sebastopol, California

We're watching Clinton's inaugural from the top of a high cliff in a national park. After it's over, we discuss how to get down (since the hill is too steep for vehicles), and how foolish it is to think that we'll get tickets to one of the balls. Later, in an interview we're watching on closed-circuit TV, Hillary Clinton says that she's going to pursue her career as a sex therapist. I think this is great. "Who would have thought?" I say. "The problem is that automatically brings up the question of Hillary and Bill's sex life, where there was never any concern about Bush's." I turn to find Bush nearby, turning away, and I run after him to apologize. I had been about to say that the only sex he'd have would be with a prostitute, and I'm glad I didn't say it.

Joan Fisher, Sleep Recorder-Interpreter for Hospitals/Poet
Age: NA
Evanston, Illinois

As a conservative Republican, I have been understandably frustrated since the election. Particularly disturbing, however, is his weekly (maybe even more often) appearances in my sleep.

Dream 1

I was on a very large plane—a 747 perhaps. The cabin was luxurious—nice big seats with lots of legroom. Toward the front I looked and standing in the aisle was Bill Clinton. He walked past me and went to a private room in the back, where the toilets are located. I followed. The room was small. It had a desk and a bed. A sink was located next to the desk. I sat in the corner and watched the President-elect. He asked me what he should do to succeed as President. I replied, "Be honest and above all don't go too far left with your economic plans."

He agreed and turned to the sink and the mirror above it. He looked into the mirror, took some paper towels, and wiped his face. As he threw away the paper towels I noticed they were grossly smudged with purplish streaks of makeup.

Dream 2

I saw Clinton near a shopping center, and I called him   a

Communist to his face. He was very angered by this insult. His face turned red. I was sure he would hit me, but he didn't.

Todd Golding, Slavic Linguist
Age: 26
Iowa City, Iowa

If I explain that my husband is a staunch Republican who can't believe that I voted for Clinton, it wouldn't take a Rhodes scholar to determine what this dream is about.

I am on a cruise ship. The public address system broadcasts a Bill Clinton speech. I wander all around the ship looking for my husband Jeff: in the lounge, around the pool, in the casino, in the restaurant. I look everywhere, but I can't find him. I ask everybody I see, but no one else has seen him either. As I approach the stern of the ship, I see Clinton. He's giving a speech. When the speech is over, I go over to him and ask, "Have you seen Jeff?"

He points out to sea and says, "He's over there."

I look and there is another cruise ship. I see Jeff waving his arms at me, and then he shouts, "Trish, get over here. You're on the wrong ship!" I try to tell him that he's the one on the wrong ship, but the wind is too strong and my words don't carry that far. He reaches out to grab my arm and pull me onto his ship, which is now right beside mine, but I don't want to go. I pull out my ticket to show him I'm on the right ship, but he says, "That's last week's ticket."

Then Clinton says, "Go if you have to. It's safer." I answer that

I don't want to be safe. I want to be right. And that's the end of the dream.

Trish Coates, Desktop Publisher
Age: 35
Royal Oak, Michigan

I was in a shopping mall–type place, at a railing in front of one of those big open places on the second floor that lets you see the first floor down below. There were people gathered around on all sides of the opening and down below, looking up. Bill Clinton was standing directly behind me, resting his chin on the top of my head as he gave a speech.

Edith Otchin McCrea, Corporate Writer
Age: 24 (just over five feet)
Chicago, Illinois

President Clinton appeared on television to talk about the economy, stupid. While speaking, he metamorphosed into his 1960s self, and his hair was rather disheveled. Later, Keith Richards of the Rolling Stones and a couple of ordinary Americans appeared and talked about how they were coping with the current economy. I must've been watching with other people, because I recall that some derogatory remarks were made—frankly, the program was not a success.

Carol A. Corbin, Secretary
Age: 49
Houston, Texas

The sequence started when I was brought by six or seven men—Secret Service—to a private train car—equipped with all the familiar articles of my work environment: an anesthesia machine, vials of drugs, blue draping towels, IV solutions, etc. I was to be the provider of anesthesia for the President's gallbladder operation. We started the procedure as the train rocked along. I was nervous and very aware of the responsibility being given to me of providing safe practice.

Relief flooded over me as he awoke and—wearing a gray shawl-like sweater—walked down the center of the aisle to a seat. He was a little dizzy and nauseated, for which I gave him a drug.

He then arose and went toward the platform at the end of the car to give a speech, and I awoke at that point with train rumbling and whistles . . . wondering what he was going to talk about and what was the hurry—and secrecy of—*surgery* by moving train.

Peggy Sharp, Certified Registered Nurse Anesthetist
Age: 43
Manchester, Missouri

I was invited to go on one of the (campaign trail) bus tours, but instead of a bus, they traveled in an airplane that taxied down the interstates. At one point, Bill approached me and asked if I wanted to go upstairs, he had something to tell me. When we got upstairs, he said, "You want to know a secret?" I said, "Sure." He said, "When I raise all those rich people's taxes? It's really going to make them mad."

Jill Draper, Full-time Mom
Age: 36
University City, Missouri

I was in a hotel room in Washington, D.C., that later turned into the Oval Office. I had been calling all day and finally got an interview with President Clinton. I was quite nervous as I tried to compose myself and get ready to ask questions. He was on the phone when I got there, so I sat on a leather chair in front of his desk. When he finally got off the phone, he told me he had to take care of something and that he'd be right back. So I left.

Amanda Thompson, Reporter
Age: 27
Kirksville, Missouri

He was giving his first State of the Union Address in my living room. I was standing just out of camera range when I suddenly and inexplicably began floating out of control to the ceiling, just moments before airtime.

Mr. Clinton was the only one tall enough to reach me, so he pulled me down by the ankle and held on to me. The only way to keep me on the ground was to hold me down, and he insisted that he be the one to do it. I was so proud sitting there on my couch with President Clinton's arm held tightly around me as the nation watched.

Jennifer Poiry, Student/Customer Service Representative
Age: 23
Leo, Indiana

I dreamed we were back at the Democratic Convention. It was my job to formally nominate Bill Clinton for President. Only I was myself, a thirty-five-year-old lawyer from St. Louis who didn't know anyone there. So I just said, "I nominate the next President of the United States, Bill Clinton," and Clinton flashed me a big grin and went up to the podium.

Pamela Triplett, Attorney
Age: 35
Chesterfield, Missouri

I was helping plan a special event of some kind where President Clinton was to attend. I was standing next to President Clinton holding a clipboard that we were both looking at. President Clinton had on a light blue polo-type shirt, a white ball cap, and a tan pair of casual pants similar to Dockers.

He was tall and tan and wore tennis shoes. We were going over a list of items on the clipboard and discussing which things would be OK'd by security and which things had to be changed.

He was standing next to me with part of his shoulder behind my arm and his arm was touching mine. Many things on the list had to be changed, but he was very kind and sexy and reassuring. His voice had that Arkansas drawl. Oh boy!

Annette Hinkle, Disc Jockey
Age: 34
Lansing, Michigan

The location is the large parking garage where a number of the World Youth Day participants are lodged. The Pope is in a makeshift bed in the open part of the garage and is surrounded by security types. Along a wall are some very small three-walled stalls in which a few people can sleep. Hillary had a stall that only allowed her enough room to sleep sitting up. Bill had one in which he had barely enough room to lie down. These three-walled stalls with the open wall at the front seemed very strange to me.

S.M.W., Collection Development Librarian
Age: 43
Boulder, Colorado

My dream took place while he was still governor. I read in the papers he would not be stopping in Phoenix. That night I dreamed he was addressing a crowd in Phoenix during his campaign. After he finished speaking and went into the building, this lovely bouquet of silk flowers floated out of a lady's hat. I grabbed the bouquet and ran up to the security guard on the steps and asked him if I could give them to Governor Clinton. He said, "No!" and grabbed them and put them in a vault.

Corey Siewert, Artist
Age: 55
Scottsdale, Arizona

I dreamed it was November 3rd and I was watching TV. The polls came on and Bill Clinton had beat George Bush. I turned to my right and saw Bill Clinton and heard him say, "Ha-ha, now I am President." He pressed a button and I heard a sound like *sweeeeee*. I looked up and saw bombs dropping. Then I saw Bill Clinton rushing into a limousine with CIA agents.

Patrick Dylan Zwick, Student
Age: 12
Salt Lake City, Utah

Elementary Bill

I have dreamt of Bill Clinton once. I am nine years old. My name is Julie Beitler. I go to school at A.D. Henderson. I dreamed that he was trying to open one of the doors in my school! No one knew he was there. So I went over to the door to help him. He turned around and I saw that it was him! I said, "Hi, I'm Julie Beitler. It is a pleasure to meet you!" I got his signature. It was a cool dream. Thank you for listening to my dream about Bill Clinton!

Julie Elizabeth Beitler, Student
Age: 9
Boca Raton, Florida

Bill Clinton appeared in my elementary school class, and I was a first-grader again. (I was in the first grade in 1961, during John F. Kennedy's presidency.) He shook my hand and said, "Thank you." It was his left hand, and his index finger was kind of "glowing." I awoke, and my immediate feeling/interpretation was that "he has the Touch" and would probably become President.

S.Y.C. (Male), Owner, Real Estate Company
Age: 38
Chicago, Illinois

While I was teaching a computer class, I realized that one of my students was Bill Clinton and that he had his Secret Service agents with him in the class. How did he know about Carole Rogers and why did he decide to take my class when he had a whole country of instructors from which to choose? I was so excited! Then I tried to calm myself down and reminded myself that he is a student, just like any other student, and he's here to learn, not as an observer. Be yourself, I thought, and teach as you normally do.

Then he asked me a question. Again, my adrenaline began to rush. When I returned to Planet Earth, I was dumbstruck that the President could ask such a basic software question. Then I realized, I teach top-level executives all the time who know a lot about many things, but when it comes to computers, they know nothing. And that is normal—so the President was just another person. I answered his question just as I would have answered anyone else.

I continued with the class until two questions came at almost the same time, one from the President, and the other from another student. The President's question came a split second before the other person's. I found myself faced with a huge dilemma—well, actually, two dilemmas. The first was that even though the President's question was first (instructors, like mothers, have a keen sense of hearing!), the other person might not have thought this was the case, and if I addressed the President's question first, the student might think I deferred to the President's question only because he was the President and therefore deserved special treatment.

Since part of being an instructor is striving to treat everyone fairly no matter who they are or their level of skill, it would be blasphemy to have one student think they were less important than another. However, the President's question did in fact come in first, and I would have to make sure that this was clear to the other student. My mind was reeling, because now that I had resolved this issue in my own mind, how would I answer the question from the President without somehow discounting all the above? I mean, how do I call on him? Mr. President? No, then the other student would for sure think that I only answered the President's question first because he is the President. No, that wouldn't work. Bill? No, that's too familiar.

The following is what I said: "Two questions came in almost at the same time; however [looking at the civilian student], the other student's question came in first, therefore I will answer his question first, and then yours. Now [looking at the President], in response to your question. . ." I was rather pleased with how I handled this potentially disastrous situation, and continued the class. Slightly before the end of class, the President and his Secret Service agents stood up and proceeded to leave the classroom.

The President smiled at me and nodded as he left. Disappointed that I didn't get the opportunity to ask him how he liked the class, I tried to ignore the sadness I felt inside. I was upset, because I didn't want to disrupt the class yet at the same time I really wanted to speak to the President personally. But I knew in my heart that he couldn't stay, because he *was* the President and had someplace to go.

Carole G. Rogers, Independent Software Instructor
Age: 37
Mountain View, California

In my dream, I went to school with my mother, who is a teacher. For some reason, I didn't have school that day but she did. She was teaching at the local middle school. I went to her classroom with her, but she forgot to bring some papers she needed. She asked me to run out to the car and get them for her. When I walked outside, a big black limousine pulled up to the front doors of the school. Bill Clinton got out of the front seat and walked right by me and into the building. I quickly followed him to see where he was going. He went into one of the classrooms, and I could see our mayor, Sophie Masloff, inside. There were other government people there, too, and they were having a secret meeting. I ran back to my mother's classroom and shouted, "Mom, the President's here!" My mom just smiled at me and said, "Oh, that's nice." Then she went back to teaching.

Patrick Tatman, Student
Age: 8
McMurray, Pennsylvania

I dreamed I was back in high school, about 1972 or '73, so we were all about sixteen or seventeen. I was sitting at my desk in a classroom when a teenaged Bill Clinton (he looked basically the same—just slimmer and younger in the face) came walking toward my desk. He was smiling and with a very obvious gesture left a folded-up note on my desk, then walked past my desk and went back to his desk. I looked at him rather puzzled and opened the note. On it, he had written, *What do you really want?*

Jean McCall, Veterinarian
Age: 37
New Orleans, Louisiana

July 11, 1993, was an important day in my life. After five hours of waiting on Waikiki Beach, Clinton arrived and gave a speech. He then shook some people's hands, but when he saw my teary eyes, he kissed mine! Here is the dream I had the following night.

Clinton was a kid my age and we liked each other. We were alone on an island with palm trees. Then, suddenly, we were walking together through a school that we had never been to before. Clinton liked heights but I didn't. We took a passageway through the school hall, and jumped on a board that had a cupboard on it. We looked below us about three hundred feet over a massive ocean. Clinton swung the cupboard door over the water and I started to fall, but he grabbed me so that I could be safe.

Jessica Kehaulani Dayan, Student
Age: 11
Fresno, California

Fast Food and Tough Questions

I was on campus and it was dusk. I was standing at the bottom of some stairs leading to a large white building. (The building had a Greek style of architecture, reminding me of a large library.) I ran up the stairs and into the building. I felt that I had to get there quickly. Once inside the building, I found myself in a cafeteria, and in front of me in the line was Bill Clinton. He had on a dark blue baseball cap. The food that was being served was barbecued ribs. I told Bill that if he was ever in San Diego, he could surely stay at my parents' house.

Later in the dream, I am sitting in my parents' house at the kitchen table and Bill Clinton is sitting across from me. I ask him if he would like something to drink, and he asks for water. As I am getting the glasses down I say to him, "All these plans sound great, but where is the money going to come from?"

Molly Graessle, Hotel Employee/Part-time Student
Age: 24
San Diego, California

My dad (who passed away in 1985) and I were sitting in his 1966 Chevrolet Impala, outside of the Chicken Box Restaurant in Pensacola, Florida, which had closed in the late seventies. We were in a very loud and heated discussion about gays in the military and equal rights. We had reached the point where there was no alternative but to say mean and hurtful things to each other.

At that moment, Bill Clinton drove up in a blue 1967 Mustang convertible. He opened his car door and stepped out. As he walked toward our car, I heard Barbra Streisand's voice come up over the loudspeaker hanging from our car door. She was singing "Woman in the Moon." During the song, Bill stopped a carhop on roller skates. He spun her around in a circle as the song finished. Then he walked up to our open car window, tapped me on the shoulder, and smiled.

> Jack W. Murphy, Child Program Supervisor,
> County Retardation Board
> Age: 38
> Sumter, South Carolina

Field Trips

It was the night before the election, and I was at my girlfriend's apartment in a plush building just above the Ogden slip. The doormen didn't like me, and I always felt odd about visiting her there. That night I couldn't sleep, and I stared out the window at the Amoco tower looming over me. I didn't know who I was going to vote for, I had just become an American citizen, and this would be my first time to vote for anything, ever. I didn't want to get it wrong. I was supposed to vote for George Bush, everything in my background pointed towards Bush, my father and brother were ardent Bush supporters. But I couldn't get over the feeling that I was making a mistake. I finally fell asleep in the hour before dawn.

In my dream, I woke up, and I was on a hillside near my parents' house in Oklahoma. It was a beautiful day, and I walked to the top of the hill, where I found Bill Clinton, in full candidate garb, spading up the earth to plant a tree. The tree was next to him: It was small, and had a net over the roots. Clinton said nothing, he didn't even look at me. He could have been alone, on the hill, sweating under the Oklahoma sun, ruining his suit and mussing up his hair. I watched him for a while, and then I looked out over at my house, but it looked like no one was home.

The next morning I drove back to my apartment in Hyde Park and voted for Bill Clinton; I told my family that I had voted for George Bush, and I have stuck with that story until now. I am not given to grandiose beliefs about the power of dreams: I think dreams are more about dinner than destiny. But I like to think that I tapped into some deep well of Zeitgeist that night, and finished at last the process of becoming an American.

A.L. (Male), Graduate Student in Economics
Age: 24
Chicago, Illinois

I was on some kind of "road trip" with a bunch of other people, including Bill. It was almost like a high school field trip, but it was all adults. My twenty-four-year-old daughter (a real Bill fan) was with me, and somehow we were included in conversations with him. He was joking around with us, making us laugh. He was very energetic. You couldn't help but want to follow him, and that's what we were doing, following him on this trip. We seemed to know what we were doing, and Clinton did, too. My daughter and I had a great time being in the entourage but I can't describe exactly what it is we were doing.

Gwenn Kelly, Business Television Consultant
Age: 47
Palos Verdes, California

Bill Clinton and I went on a walking tour of the United States. We were dressed in hiking boots, shorts, flannel shirts, backpacks, etc. Our plan was to walk up the East Coast of the U.S., then head west across the northern states, south down the Pacific Coast, then east to return to our starting point. The idea was for us to meet lots of people around the country, and to get their input on how to solve our problems.

I can't remember meeting any people though, just walking and enjoying the countryside, and becoming very good friends with Bill Clinton. The dream did not last for our whole journey. It ended with us climbing an incredibly steep, rough trail in the Rocky Mountains. Near the top of the trail, there appeared to be an opening to a cave. When Bill Clinton and I entered, it turned out to be a fantastic museum. It displayed art, minerals, wildlife, everything! It was very modern, and there were many other people looking at all of the exhibits. I woke up pleased that Bill Clinton and I spent many hours browsing through the museum, soaking up knowledge like a sponge absorbs water.

Christine Eaton, Ph.D., Elementary School
Physical Education Teacher
Age: 40
Phoenix, Arizona

With several friends, I am viewing an open, grassy area. It is very sunny and the grass is brown, giving a golden (California-like) quality. There is a large brick house at the edge of this open area. Turns out it's the Governor's Mansion in Little Rock. Bill Clinton is at the window. Seeing us, he smiles and invites us in.

Once inside (this part is fuzzy), he asks if anyone knows how many phone calls per hour come in—either to or about the Ku Klux Klan. I guess something between 550 and 750. Bill says, "It's 769—and Hillary guessed it." He was so pleased with this. The words "policy wonk" come up for me. Then we're leaving the mansion and piling into the backseat of a small car—probably a VW "bug." Bill is in the driver's seat, and we're waiting for the front-seat passenger, Hillary. Then we all drive off together smiling.

Linda C. Wilson, Clerical Social Worker
Age: 53
San Francisco, California

I was staying at a rustic Northwoods lake resort. The Clintons were staying there, too. Bill was studying cartography and fishing for relaxation purposes. Bill and I became friends. Hillary jealously confronted him, but he honestly denied any wrongdoing. He essentially dared her to set a trap for me. He silently hoped I would have the wits to avoid inflaming her jealousy and suspicions.

I was walking down a dirt path on my way to meet him when Hillary popped out of her hiding place in the woods. I was uncomfortable in her presence, since Bill had confided in me that he intended to leave her. She tried to act casually while asking her leading and insinuating questions. I acted casually, too. I pretended to be distracted from her questions by the task of counting the change in my pockets. I repeatedly miscounted and started over until I reached the safety of the lodge. I casually said goodbye and left her standing, somewhat taken aback, on the path.

L.L.M. (Female), Employee Benefits Specialist
Age: NA
Roseville, Minnesota

Bill and Hillary Clinton and I were in a rural setting. A small college was located here. There was a discussion about moving one of the departments of the college to another part of the grounds. We left the area we were in, and I went one way and they another. I took what turned out to be a shortcut to the place I wanted to go. It was on the other side of some trees and had a small lake. I recall thinking to myself, "Why not put the Sciences here near the lake?" Eventually, the Clintons found me and we discussed my ideas. The name of the college was something like Ward College or Word College. Upon my aerial departure, I noticed how sparsely populated the area near the college was.

The scene shifted and I was with the Clintons in a home or office area. Hillary wanted me to do her hair and put it in a French twist. I explained that I didn't do hair very well. This comment didn't seem to stop her from wanting me as some type of aide to her. I felt that this was a great honor, since her husband was being elected President.

S.M.W., Collection Development Librarian
Age: 43
Boulder, Colorado

I dreamed that my six-year-old son and myself were waiting for friends to finish working out at a local health spa. This holistic, private-club–type spa was closing, since it was the Thursday before the Fourth of July holiday. One of the attendants told my son and me to go ahead and enjoy the mineral "green baths," and led us to this steamy room. I said, "Thank you!"

We had this whole green place to ourselves, replete with Japanese gardens, music, soft lighting, and exotic orchids all around us. Then a Secret Service man with dark glasses and a man with a towel entered through the steam. The Secret Service man motioned to me, "Shhh," and I nodded. And there, fifty yards or so away, was Bill Clinton, in the same room as we were. When my son noticed, he got excited and said, "Mommy, look! He looks like the President of the United States!"

I started laughing, and said that it was, and told him to act naturally and stay calm. We were exhilarated, yet we had to contain our excitement. The Secret Service men came over to me and explained in monotone voices that we were to keep this to ourselves if at all possible. They said it was "imperative" to remain "hush-hush" about this. Of course, I was blushing and nervous and nodded and promised I would do as they asked. When they left the room, an attendant asked how we enjoyed the green room with the "surprise guest," and we laughed together.

Valiana Parr, Student/Homemaker
Age: 38
Virginia Beach, Virginia

Dreams of Bill

I was riding my bike in the town of Clintonville, a real town near my hometown. I rode my bike past several old houses towards Interstate 80 when I looked over and there sat Bill Clinton on the steps of the porch of one of the old houses. He was dressed very casually, in jeans and a sweatshirt. It was summer.

I stopped and said, "Hey, aren't you Bill Clinton?" Bill said, "Yes, but keep it quiet. We are traveling incognito and don't want to attract crowds." He was very friendly and polite. He said that the girls were up the street at the local gas station, which happens to be owned and operated by Sikh immigrants from India, filling up the station wagon. They were on their way to Grove City, PA. where he was giving a speech at a local Kiwanis Club. I thought how ironic it was that Bill Clinton would find himself in a town called Clintonville.

He wished me well as an old, dusty station wagon pulled up to the house and he hopped in. The vehicle turned left onto Route 208 towards Grove City, and I pedaled my bike in the same direction. All of a sudden, Hillary began waving her arm out of the passenger side window for me to pedal faster and to catch up. The car then turned left onto the Clinton-Irwin Gun Club Road, an unpaved, dirt road. They stopped and Bill, Hillary, and Chelsea all got out. Bill walked towards the front of the car and out of sight. Much to my surprise, Hillary handed me a lit marijuana joint and smoked it. I exclaimed excitedly, "So Bill really does inhale." Hillary shot back quickly, "Oh no! Bill doesn't get high. He doesn't like it. But me and Chelsea do."

Ed Rollins, Rehabilitation Counselor
Age: 40
Kennerdell, Pennsylvania

Friend of the Family

Bill Clinton knocked at the door of our home. When I opened the door, he said, "I'm here to congratulate you on the birth of your first grandchild."

I was so surprised to see him and recall saying, "How did you know?"

He replied, "I have a way of knowing everything." We were both shaking hands and congratulating each other.

I don't know why, but after having this dream, I felt very strongly that our first grandchild would be born earlier than expected; be a girl; and that Bill Clinton would win the election as President.

Our granddaughter was born on November 3, 1993, Election Day, and my daughter named her Chelsea. We were thrilled—a new granddaughter and a new President all in one day.

Doris Galisin, Secretary
Age: 51
Pittsburgh, Pennsylvania

Bill and Hillary were at a family gathering. People were rushing around getting ready to go somewhere. I wondered what they thought of our family. They had been telling funny stories about someone else's family. They referred to my eighty-something-year-old cousin Henrietta by her first name as if they knew her. At first they were not talking. Bill was leaning against a wall. Hillary was sitting in the last row of an auditorium. I couldn't decide if I should get my camera and take pictures of them with our family the way we had in 1979 when Abba Eban was over. I wanted to act instead like it was natural for them to be there.

Finally, my aunt started asking Hillary questions about her health policy. Hillary explained it candidly and articulately. My aunt asked if she had teams set up all over the country. Then a larger question was asked and I thought Bill would answer it, but Hillary did instead. Meanwhile, I was trying to collect money to return to the Iowa Writers' Workshop, from where I graduated ten years ago. It now cost eighteen hundred dollars a day. Bill still said nothing and stood against a wall. They sat on opposite sides of the room.

Dina Elenbogen
Age and Occupation: NA
Chicago, Illinois

I received a call from a White House staff member: Chelsea wants to come stay with my girlfriend and me (we have a large apartment). She is tired of all the attention and just wants to hang around New York with us, watch TV, play with our dog and be a regular kid for a couple of weeks. Who am I to say no? Almost immediately, however, the press sniffs us out. They start annoying the doormen. They start hounding me when I go out jogging, with questions about what Chelsea had for breakfast, etc. As each hour passes, the media people become more numerous; the local TV station news trucks park on our corner, they lay cables and have glaring lights everywhere. We get another call from the White House that they need to get Chelsea out, but they don't know how. And, of course, Chelsea doesn't want to leave; she likes us and loves the dog (a toy Yorkshire terrier). Finally, I bring her, protesting and whining, down the service elevator to the building garage, and we attempt to drive directly out. But we are stopped at the garage entrance by a Secret Service man who says that we don't have the proper clearance.

Elliot Essman, Writer/Lecturer/Publisher
Age: 43
New York, New York

I just happened to be with them (the Clintons)—this time at a beautiful, Roman-style resort home with gardens, fountains, pools, etc. I'm just "there"—not really a guest or even speaking with them, but a woman friend of mine in the dream is their "daughter." We just enjoy the day and the scene—it's like we've got carte blanche to the place; however, nothing real significant happens.

Tony Garry, Self-employed Musician
Age: 41
St. Paul, Minnesota

I dreamt of the President and his wife and daughter. In my dream, Chelsea was a baby around one year old. They were at a friend's, cooking out, playing horseshoes, and basically interacting as family friends. I was keeping an eye on Chelsea and visiting with the President and his wife.

Other friends were dropping in and I would meet them in the driveway, telling them of the President's visit.

Janice Allen, Housewife
Age: 33
Gillespie, Illinois

At my current age, I was back in my bedroom at my childhood family home. I was curled up on my twin bed with a female Secret Service agent on duty with her two-way radio. George Stephanopoulos was asleep curled up on my other twin bed. Everyone around us was asleep. Bill was sitting up in his sleeping bag on the floor in the corner of my bedroom at the foot of my bed. We were the only people up, and we stayed up all night just talking about the issues of the campaign. Sort of my own personal "town meeting"!

Kimberly Dale, TV Production Assistant
Age: 38
Arden, North Carolina

Bill, Hillary, and I are very close friends. Much of our time is spent together, and Hillary and I are like the closest of sisters. There is lots of fun and laughter among us three. Suddenly, things turn sad. Hillary becomes seriously ill and dies. Bill and I are standing, crying on each other's shoulders. Bill looks at me and says, "How will I ever go on without Hillary?"

I tell Bill, "It will be okay. . .I will marry you." Somehow I know this is what Hillary would want me to do.

Callie Daniel, Housewife
Age: 41
Yoder, Indiana

He was present at our family reunion in Ferrum, Virginia. He acted like he belonged there. He was walking around with a glass in his hand, talking to everyone as if he was one of us.

Guerlain Boyd, Owner, Gerry's Cleaning Service
Age: 57
Charlotte, North Carolina

Bill Clinton and I along with my father were all traveling (in a truck) through green rolling hills at dusk. The whole dream was Bill and I trying to get comfortable in the cramped cab area to go to sleep.

A second dream was about Bill being the facilitator during a family argument. No one wanted to listen to Bill but me.

Angel Poole, College Student, Senior Level
Age: N/A
New Orleans, Louisiana

Bill Clinton and his coworkers and staff (about twenty people and mostly men) visited my home. They were having a very relaxed time enjoying the good food, sitting in my backyard taking life easy, really enjoying the fellowship—not especially with me—but with each other. They seemed to be taking care of business without the fear of press and other critics.

All of a sudden, one of my friends drove up unannounced, and Bill said, "What is she doing here?" I told him I didn't know she was coming. He seemed put out. He had told me no one else was supposed to be here—as if I had promised him no one else would come.

Dorothy Brunson, Retired Schoolteacher (39 years)
Age: 69
Houston, Texas

Hillary, Bill, and I were riding down the road in a Lincoln Town Car. Of course, Hillary was driving and Bill and I were in the back. When we stopped, Bill got out, went to the back of the car, and opened the trunk. He told Chelsea, who was in the fetal position and tied up, that they would let her out of the trunk only after she was finished with puberty. He said she was ruining his chances for the '96 election, then he slammed the trunk and got back in the back and told Hillary to go ahead.

Shelby Weddle, College Student
Age: 17
Springhill, Louisiana

I was walking—or standing—somewhere more like an immobile situation. (I'm just getting over a second hip operation.) Bill had grown a red and gray beard of about three inches on his chin, and his hair was longer around his ears. He was wearing a cotton elbow-length short-sleeve shirt. It was plaid—brown and yellow and some white. I think we were in Hot Springs, Arkansas. He touched my right arm. I asked him, "How's your mother?" and he was perfectly quiet. I didn't say anything else to him, and he didn't say anything to me that I can recall. But I can still feel his hand on my arm!

I feel close to him without ever having met him. He was raised in Hot Springs, which is one of my hometowns. He was my mother's paper boy. The church he belonged to you could see from my front porch. I have a son that's Bill's age—Bill is one month older to the day. I get the feeling from my realistic dream that I will really meet him.

Myrillyn M. Zweig
Age: 71
Chapel Hill, North Carolina

It was all very normal. Bill and Hillary were still in their work clothes, as they didn't have time to change into T-shirts and jeans. They had just come straight from the White House.

We were standing on the porch of our cottage, discussing plain vacation stuff like cooking hamburgers and hiking. It was the very beginning of a pleasant week. My husband and I were not overwhelmed by their presence, we were just glad to be with them. It was like seeing old friends or family members that you've been parted from for too long.

Leslie Carroll, Purchasing Agent, U.S. Army Corps of Engineers
Age: 33
Huntington, West Virginia

Guess Who's Coming to Dinner

I was eating Thanksgiving dinner in the dining room of my dead grandma's tiny house in Greenville, Illinois. My grandma was a fiendishly good cook, and the table was groaning with food. Turkey, giant bowls of mashed potatoes, creamed corn, candied sweet potatoes, cranberry-orange sauce, pumpkin *and* apple pie with Cool Whip, cloverleaf rolls, the whole Thanksgiving bit. My mother and little sister were at the table with me. And so was my crazy, opinionated, straight-ticket-Democrat, white-haired Grandma Wise, who is quite dead.

We were all eating furiously and conversing with our holiday guest, who happened to be Bill Clinton. It was a lively, comfortable, easy dinner conversation. My grandma and mother kept looking admiringly at the governor of Arkansas and touching his hand every once in a while. I remember being amused at the extraordinary amount of food he consumed while sitting there. My sister and I exchanged glances and giggled about this. There was an overall feeling of comfort and pleasure of a cozy domestic sort.

My father, who is very shy, was lurking, as usual, in the kitchen, raiding my grandma's cookie jar, which was shaped like an enormous red porcelain apple. He never joined the conversation, but I could see out of the corner of my eye that he was listening and smiling in between bites of cookie. I woke up feeling absolutely peaceful and happy.

I voted for Bill Clinton the next day because I firmly believe my grandma (more of a Democrat than Roosevelt, Truman, Kennedy, and George McGovern all rolled into one) paid me a visit from the grave to give Clinton her personal stamp of approval. Plus, he liked her cooking. She was flattered.

Susan Wise, Artist and Illustrator
Age: 34
Chicago, Illinois

He came to my apartment and complimented the decoration and the fact that I had managed to save my paintings (I am an artist by hobby) from Hurricane Andrew. I started telling him everything that happened the night of the storm; however, I noticed that the now First Lady was looking bored sitting by herself in my living room. I thought she might get jealous of me, so I grabbed the President's arm and walked over to join her. The strange part is that my dream seemed very real and logical. I offered them drinks and appetizers on my new black china, and I even poured some cheap vodka into an empty bottle of Absolut to make things look a little more elegant.

About a week later, after he won the election, I started dreaming about him repeatedly. Some dreams were simple conversations about the inauguration, ecology, and his plans. We even discussed Ross Perot. In several of my dreams, Al Gore would drop in on our conversation. In one of them, the Vice President asked me where "the little boys' room" was, so I asked President Clinton to discourage him from going to the bathroom, because there were no clean towels in the house.

Sometimes, I found myself joking with the President and even gossiping as if we were old friends. There were a couple of dreams in which we were getting openly sexual and I was trying my best to seduce him. He seemed pleased.

Maria F. Martinez, Stress Management Consultant
Age: 43
Miami, Florida

The President and Hillary were at my parents' house, and Hillary was in the living room with some family members, having a good time, laughing and hugging!

Bill was sitting at the dining room table talking to my parents. My mother had called them up and asked them to come over. She wanted to express her concern about the way women were being treated in Southeast Asia!

I couldn't believe it when I saw the President there! I was so excited I had tears swelling in my eyes. My father told me to "dry up."

"Don't you know the President is going to everyone's house to hear their views on different subjects?"

No, I didn't know, but when I awoke I did think it was a good idea!

Yvonne Myers, Housewife/College Student
Age: 33
Brighton, Michigan

The President is coming to Livonia, and my home is chosen for his visit. Here is my reaction:

"Why me? Now why not Woodcox, they've been here since Revolution (time second house from me, down the road)? "Maybe because I am from Macedonia, and he would like an opinion how he is going to be judged in my country?

"No problem, we will make pita with lots of cheese, eggs, and spinach, and maybe stuffed peppers with ground beef and rice, and tasty chicken soup. He will drink a glass of wine, that goes smooth with this kind of food . . . .

"I don't know what we are going to talk about, but I'll be careful on my English, so that he'll no doubt notice my accent, but I'll go with regular, understandable English.

"Now, how about sleeping for the night. If he is only by himself, we'll give him Eric's (my youngest son's) bedroom, which is thirteen feet by sixteen feet. The boy goes on a couch in the living room. But if Mrs. Clinton is with him, we are going to ask Marie (next house to us to the north, and last on a half-mile, dead-end street). They have brand-new house, with beautiful bedroom, including bath and toilet, and Clintons will also be thrilled by Italian hospitality . . . .

"Man, Alekso, is this a dream, what an honor for us poor people!" And I started crying. I awoke scared-like, my head sweating, my eyes wet . . . Realized was a dream, but I was kind of honored to have such a dream that made me cry for a little more until I fell asleep to rest the remaining time . . . and go to work.

Alexander N. Mark, Engineering Draftsman
Age: 63
Livonia, Michigan

We lived in a big farmhouse way out in the country. We farmed, and had several acres of land with a big river running through one of our fields. One evening we were sitting on our front porch, and the President, his wife, and four of their body-guards came up in the yard. They had been walking and looked very tired. They had car trouble, so they came to our house to try to get someone to fix it. We couldn't help them with the car, but I invited them to a big country supper. Afterwards, they said that was the best meal they had ever eaten in their lives.

President Clinton asked what we did around here for enter-tainment. We told him we went fishing in the river across the field to our left. He said he'd like to go, but his wife just wanted to stay on the porch where it was cool. He talked her into going anyway, so we all walked across the field to the river. I gave the President my rod and reel to fish with, but when we got to the river, it was just about dried up. There had always been a big river there, but now we couldn't even fish. I just told them I didn't know what happened, because we had fished there about every evening, and it was a huge river.

We walked back up across the field toward the house, and I woke up, wondering what happened to all that river water. The President didn't seem to mind being out in the country with us, but his wife seemed so bored.

Shirley C. Bennett, Computer Technician
Age: 57
Walnut Cove, North Carolina

I had jogged to a friend's house to say hello. She was busy preparing a postinaugural dinner for President Clinton that her parents (who are actually Republicans) were hosting. Nobody had arrived yet, so I wandered around the dining room admiring the festive decor and beautiful table settings. Suddenly, Bill emerged from the guest bathroom wearing his workout clothes. He invited me to attend the dinner party as his date. I immediately pictured my name and photo across the tabloids as the home-wrecker who had destroyed the President's family and career. I quickly declined, under the pretense that I had nothing with me to wear and needed to freshen up. He persisted and I panicked, running out of the house without any explanation to anyone.

Lisa Langlois, Assistant Manager, M.I.S. Department
Age: 26
St. Louis, Missouri

My dream involved an invitation to the Clintons' home for dinner. All I remember is that I was seated at the kitchen table with Hillary and a bunch of children. Bill was at the stove, cooking, of all things, fried green tomatoes. He was on the phone all the time that I was there.

Kimberly Davis, Assembler/Student
Age: 27
St. Louis, Missouri

Hand-holding, Handshakes, and Hugs

Bill Clinton and entourage were appearing in my town. I walked past him as he sat at a small table in what seemed to be a school basement. I told him I would like very much to prepare breakfast for him. He cheerfully and graciously accepted, so I hurried to prepare it for him. I cooked pancakes, all of which turned out thick and fluffy. I folded one of them over, like an omelette.

I hurried to serve my creation to the President. Other workers were now scurrying around to serve those attending this meal with the President. I pushed past a dark-haired girl who was preparing to serve the President. I told her I had worked hard to prepare these pancakes, and "I just *have* to be the one to serve him. I just *have to be!*" I moved in and slid my pancake onto the President's plate, whereupon the pancake was no longer big and fluffy, but a dark, hard, crisp disk. I decided to serve it anyway. No one reacted. It was as if the pancake was fine. The President continued talking with those seated around him.

The next thing I knew, I was in a crowd waiting outside a church door—it appeared to be a side church door, perhaps one leading off the sanctuary. We in the crowd were waiting for the President to appear. Someone official announced the President; but suddenly, a stranger (but official-looking) came out of the church. The crowd sighed together in disappointment. The next second, however, the President was announced and Bill Clinton came out of the church door. He proceeded down a small set of steps—four or five—and made his way down the sidewalk of the church. I managed to walk along the sidewalk in even stride with the President. Suddenly, he was holding my hand, not as two people strolling along might hold hands, but in a clinging way—mid-torso height. Clinging, clinging almost as if each wanted to continue clinging, but knew that it wasn't possible.

As President Clinton entered a building nearby, we each reluctantly released our grip. The feeling was that neither wanted to stop holding hands, but that it was necessary.

Patricia Fleming, High School Teacher
Age: 48
St. Peters, Missouri

My dream took place in a McDonald's (what a surprise!) and Bill was there with his entourage. Of course, people were swarming around him and he was shaking hands with whomever asked. At first, I thought I would stand back (since I am not normally an autograph seeker of any kind, and after all, just being in the same room with a President of the U.S. is exciting enough in itself), but then I thought, "No, I really am impressed with this man and I want him to know it!"

In the dream, I did request a handshake and was absolutely thrilled when I received one. I felt as though Bill and I had made some sort of connection.

Allyson C. Hitt, Cartographer
Age: 24
Berkeley, California

I dreamed about this large helicopter landing. The man who got out was Bill Clinton. He came over and kneeled down on one knee and put his arm around my eight-year-old grandson, Brandon Marshall. He had that sweet, kind expression on his face as he does in real life.

He was talking to my grandson as if Brandon was some kind of hero. I must have woke up because the dream ended.

Marie C. Marshall, Retired Licensed Practical Nurse
Age: 78
Hillsville, Virginia

I dreamed that I was dancing with President Bill Clinton at a party. The crowd around us was very joyous, the atmosphere relaxed and the music very Latin American.

I asked the President why he had chosen to dance with me, an older woman badly dressed and coiffed and unknown to him, and he replied, "Because you're the only person here tonight who looks sad, and I want to know if I can help."

My eyes flooded with tears at his kindness, and I blurted out, "I want to work. I need to work and no one will hire me. I am a desperate human being." The President stopped dancing for a while and, with an affectionate smile and tone, said, "Consider yourself employed. Hillary has a position available and I know that she will like you and hire you." Then we resumed the dance.

The dream faded away before I could ask about the position, but I woke up feeling much more confident about my future.

Liliane Dennis, Unemployed at the Moment
Age: 58
Denver, Colorado

I am a new immigrant, originally from the Philippines. I came in September 1992. I've always liked George Bush, primarily because of his fatherly personality. I didn't know Bill Clinton until one night, two weeks before the election, when I dreamt about him. I told my husband about my dream, and he started laughing at me because, he thought, I was weird to dream of Bill Clinton, of all people. There was something inside me that made me think that Bill Clinton is my soul mate, because the dream didn't happen once, but for five consecutive nights. I felt so uneasy because the dream was so real.

It was kind of dark, and Bill and I were in our jogging outfits. My dream told me that we were more than friends, as we were holding hands walking from the church. We were members of a church choir. Bill seemed to be a very ordinary man, but he told me about his dreams for America, like improving the standard of living and education. I was just listening intently and felt sadness in my heart because I had the feeling that he would become President and we would not be able to do the things that we enjoyed, like singing and jogging.

The following night, I again dreamt of Bill. He had been elected President, but I still saw him as the ordinary Bill, full of sincerity and honesty. The important thing was not that he was the President. The dream showed him as ordinary, sincere, and having a lot of love for the country. The same sort of dreams were replayed to me for two more nights, until the last night, when I finally asked Bill this: "Bill, now that you're President, will I ever see you again?"

His reply was very positive, but vague, something like, "Someday we'll sing together, and no matter what, you'll always be in my heart."

These dreams were so vivid that I really believe, even now, that Bill Clinton is a soul mate, and somehow I'm hoping that when he sees me in a crowd—not that I'll ever have a chance—he'll recognize me.

> Mariam N. Rafiq, Homemaker
> Age: 42
> San Jose, California

I dreamed I was riding face-to-face with Hillary in a limousine. I woke up shortly after, thought about what a strange dream it was, and then fell back to sleep. Then I dreamed I was at the inaugural parties in D.C., and Bill Clinton came out and shook my hand.

The only other political personality I've ever dreamed of was George Bush, shortly before a visit from my mother-in-law. The Clinton dream left me more cheerful, and even inspired me to write a letter to Hillary about health care.

Katherine DeVine, Artist/Mother
Age: 35
Roanoke, Virginia

I dreamed I was on the beach at night in the rain. I was making some sort of speech from a podium in front of hundreds of rain-soaked people who were sitting on the sand. Behind me stood Bill (to my left) and Hillary (to my right).

When I was finished speaking, I turned to Bill, who was wearing a dress shirt (no tie) with his sleeves rolled up, and we embraced tearfully and joyfully for quite a while as Hillary looked on. I also remember thinking that Hillary was not as pretty in person.

D.J.W. (Female), Writer
Age: 23
Bloomfield, New Jersey

I'm outside my local McDonald's and there's a big crowd. I know the President is inside. I can't wait to meet him, but can't get inside because there are so many people in the way. Then I think I see him walking out. So I go up to him and introduce myself, only it isn't Bill. It's just a man who looks like him. I'm embarrassed. Two more times, men who look like Clinton walk out, I think each is the Prez, but then realize that they aren't. Each time,

I'm more frustrated and embarrassed. Then the crowd starts moving forward in parade-march fashion. Knowing that Bill will be marching along with them, I start walking in the opposite direction inside the crowd till I see Clinton. He is surrounded by a circle of people, laughing and shaking hands. I put out my hand and say, "Hi, Bill." He laughs out loud, takes my hand, pulls me closer, and gives me a one-armed hug around the shoulder. "I told y'all that people would start calling me Bill," he laughs. "I hope you don't mind," I say, "I didn't mean any disrespect. Jimmy Carter prefers being called Jimmy. . . ." "No! I love it," Clinton says, then steps on some steps to give a speech. I don't remember what he was saying at this point, but I soon said, "Do us proud, Bill." When I did, he stopped his speech to answer, "I will."

Mike W. Sheets, Machinist
Age: 31
Dublin, Virginia

Bill Clinton and I were playing catch in the backyard (it seems like it was probably my backyard someplace, but I didn't recognize it). We were having a really good time, and were very informal with each other (he was Bill and I was Mary). Then he said it was time for him to go. I remember we were both sad and cried and hugged each other. I had the impression I would never see him again.

M.D., Word Processor
Age: 47
Imperial Beach, California

I dreamt that President Bill Clinton and I were close personal friends.

We were walking along the beach with a view of a splendid massive ocean. We were in a sunny location but I'm not even sure if we were in the United States. He told me how he planned to prioritize domestic and foreign affairs. He walked with his arm around me. We were very intimate friends (not sexual at all). I confirmed that he had made honorable decisions.

Later we stopped by a married couple's home and visited with their children. The President and I were obviously mutual friends of the family. The members of the family were very attractive. Their nationality was not readily identifiable. They all had beautiful brown complexions and curly hair.

The President and I sat next to each other in the couple's modest apartment. All of the walls were a rich marigold yellow. We let the children climb all over our laps (there must have been at least four children ranging from three to ten years old). We laughed and played and talked for about an hour.

It was so nice to visit the family, because the President and I were safe from the media. We could hug and talk with each other genuinely, without our affectionate actions being misconstrued.

Later, we left the apartment in separate cars. We knew we would see each other again; however, we made no plans. We only gave each other a long goodbye hug and enjoyed the fact that we could be so real with one another.

Valerie Ramdin, Research Associate
Age: 27
Chicago, Illinois

I'll call him Bill and not Mr. Clinton or Mr. President, because in my dream he was a friend of the family.

It was during the campaign and he was walking around my quiet suburban neighborhood, going house to house, talking with people. He had on his sweats and a red T-shirt like when he's out jogging. He came to my house. I was hugging him like I hadn't seen him in a long time. After I gave him some lemonade, Bill, my husband, and I just had casual conversation about how the election was going. I felt very good vibrations from this visit. He said he'd return after the election, he'd see us later, and off he went. I don't know why I dreamt about him. My husband and I were for Perot. But after the dream, I just had a good feeling about him: That he is honest, sincere, and genuine.

T.T. (Female), Homemaker
Age: 25
Margate, Florida

I dreamed that President Clinton was in Detroit for a convention or something and he was staying at a hotel on the river. I really wanted to see him, and so did another girl I used to work with named Hillary Tullio. (Honest!) It was like a competition to see who could get there first and who Bill would choose. The hotel room he was staying in was high up, and there were guards all around the building.

I remember there were guard dogs who would attack me if I got near them. I got up on the windowsill by swinging from a rope on another building. When I got there, he was already on his way downstairs, where the other girl was waiting. He was coming down a huge staircase with velvet steps wearing his pajama bottoms (no shirt), carrying the newspaper and a cup of coffee. I ran up to him and hugged him. I remember that his chest was really muscular and I thought he was so handsome and sexy. I started to kiss him. . .then unfortunately (or fortunately maybe from another's point of view), I woke up.

Gretchen Linenger, Flower Shop Manager
Age: 27
Troy, Michigan

I am sitting on a couch next to Bill. Members of my family are seated in the room. We are attending my sister's wedding, and guests are visiting throughout the house. My hands are ice-cold, so I slip one of them into Bill's. (I know he is my husband, but I can't remember being with him before.) Then he takes my other hand as if to warm them both in his large hands. He continues to visit with the others in the room. I think how nice it is to have someone to be close to who feels the same way about you.

Then Bill looks at me. He moves forward slightly and turns toward me, giving me room to slide down on the couch. He bends over me as if to kiss me, but he hesitates. Both of our mouths are very dry, and we are trying to work up a little saliva before we kiss. At this point in the dream, the scene switches, and Bill is no longer a part of it.

Tricia Ann Heliker, Office Manager
Age: 47
St. Louis, Missouri

Susan (my lover) and I are staying in an old (but nice) hotel in a city. When going back to our room, we attempt to take a short-cut through the building's twin (but even more elegant, larger, with statues and sculptures on the exterior walls).

Before we even enter, a woman sternly and disapprovingly blocks our path, saying, "This building is for registered persons only." Basically, she was telling us common folk were not permitted to enter.

So we start to cross the street to our own building, but find a large crowd assembling on the street. Susan goes on ahead. But I happen to look up at "our" hotel (the one we're approaching), and I see that President Clinton has come out onto one of the balconies to make a speech! "Wow!" I say to myself. I signal Susan to come back.

Then we attempt to move closer to shake Bill's hand (he has moved down to the street now). There are police officers with guns ready, poised to protect the President. I am a bit nervous, but I press on. The crowd seems to split. I go toward the left. I find myself in front of Hillary! She shakes my hand *firmly*. I stumble for words and say, "Nice to meet you." I am thrilled as Susan and I walk up to our room.

Sandy Kuntz, Educator
Age: 27
San Diego, California

I was in an atmosphere of much energy. People were discussing matters of great importance, milling around a large room. I saw Bill and we shook hands and looked each other in the eyes and I said to him, "You're going to win, Bill." He acknowledged me with a look. His eyes said, "Thank you," and then I awoke.

My feeling is that President Clinton has an accessible spirit, so to speak, and it is very easy to call it in.

I've never dreamed of a President before, or any other politician for that matter. Once I dreamed that I passed Nancy Reagan on the freeway in L.A., and told her she should have hired me instead, but I suppose that's not unusual given my occupation!

Rosemary Taylor, Astrological Consultant
Age: 40
Lansing, Michigan

I was sitting in the bleachers at school. Everyone was there waiting for President Clinton to come into the gym. He had come to visit our school. I was at the very end near the door. All of a sudden, the President, Hillary, and Al Gore walked into the gym. They were standing right next to me. The only problem was that Al Gore had the head of George Bush (but I knew it was Al). I shook hands with President Clinton and then I woke up.

L.N.M., Sophomore in High School
Age: 15 1/2
Fenton, Missouri

I had stopped at a gas station and noticed a commercial bus was in the lot. I saw a crowd of people and then realized that it was the Clinton/Gore bus. I rushed toward the crowd and saw Hillary and Clinton. I did not hesitate to walk past everyone and I mentally decided to call out "Bill," and he turned toward me. I held out my right hand for a handshake, and he responded. I remember that when he took my hand, he moved toward me. I don't recall that I said anything specific or that he responded with anything specific. I just remember thinking, "Please help us; we need a strong leader in this country." What was significant is that his hand was so big, and so warm to the touch. I felt he was really "touching" me—using my hand as a conduit to my mind—giving me a sense of security and warmth I have rarely felt in a handshake. I remember bringing my left hand up and holding his hand between mine. Then he let go and moved on through the crowd. I walked back to my car. When I awoke from the dream, I felt so wonderful, so peaceful.

> **Vicki Pettus, Manager for a State Agency for Recycling**
> **Age: 42**
> **Frankfort, Kentucky**

I was at a music convention in a large hotel. I got separated from my group, and I got lost in a back stairwell. There I saw Bill Clinton with some Secret Service agents. He was leaning back against a wall with his head down, obviously upset.

I walked up to him and he looked into my eyes. I gave him a tight hug and told him that everything was going to work out and that we knew he was doing his best. He held on to me and said, "Thank you," like he was really relieved. I stepped back, and he smiled and held both my hands. Then I went down the hallway to find my meetings.

> **S.S. (Female), Band Teacher**
> **Age: 30**
> **Valley Park, Missouri**

Hillary in Charge

My boyfriend and I were going over to the Clintons' for dinner. Only the White House wasn't the White House. It was still on Pennsylvania Avenue, but it was this small, quaint two-story Southern-type house. Bill was all nervous because he was going to go on TV later. He was in his usual blue suit, and he had tons of pancake makeup on his face. His face sort of looked like one of those plastic masks of former Presidents that they sell in novelty shops. (Chelsea and Socks were nowhere to be seen.) Hillary was dressed pretty casual—blue stretch pants and a long sweatshirt. But she was definitely in charge.

Bill was floundering around, worried about his makeup, the kinds of questions the reporters might ask him, whether dinner was good enough for us (my boyfriend is a chef), as they were serving Southern-fried chicken, mashed potatoes, and gravy. . .but Hillary was in charge. The phones (there were many) kept ringing, and she would answer the inquiries calmly and directly. Aides kept coming in with papers to be signed, and she would sign Bill's name to them. Bill was basically worthless and it became pretty obvious that Hillary was the brains behind the operation and was calling all the shots. But she was sort of a benevolent-dictator type—handling Bill almost as you would a temperamental child—indulging his delusions, etc.

Karen Therese, Desktop Publisher
Age: 32
Seattle, Washington

I saw a very large (she seemed large because I was smaller than usual in my dream) Hillary Clinton surrounded by advisers in suits, conferring intensely. Finally, after much heated discussion, they pulled out a suitcase, from which Hillary took a perfect, doll-sized Bill with a key in his back. Hillary set him on his feet, wound up the key, and sent him on his way with a pat on the bottom.

Iran Narges, First-Year University Student
Age: NA
Chicago, Illinois

I'm sitting in a shopping mall with Bill and Hillary, and I have the Sunday paper (comics on top) spread out in front of me. Bill is on my right, with not much room to sit, and Hillary is on my left. I turn to Hillary and begin to tell her my theory about the way the human memory works, and she turns to me in a snotty tone and says, "All you want to do is ride in on someone else's coattails."

Ethan Winograd, Bartender
Age: NA
Pittsburgh, Pennsylvania

I was on the Clintons' staff. They were relaxing in a large athletic center. It was quiet, since there were few people there. I had to report to Hillary and walked over to meet her as she relaxed by the indoor pool. All she had on was a bikini bottom and a pair of sunglasses which were perched on her head as she read something obviously important. I was naked and carried a clipboard. Hillary was annoyed at having her reading interrupted. She asked me what I wanted and added that I was not supposed to be naked at that particular time (but the implication was that at other times nudity among the staff was encouraged).

Before I could answer, Bill jogged in. He was wearing one of those casual tennis outfits you see in 1930s movies: long white pants, sneakers, preppy tennis sweater with the piping around the neck. He seemed happy-go-lucky but he, too, froze under Hillary's annoyed glare. Without concluding any business, Bill and I walked off.

Elliot Essman, Writer/Lecturer/Publisher
Age: 43
New York, New York

I was in a large crowd of people when someone said the President is coming. I turned and told them I just wish I could visit with him and explain how ordinary people feel. In the next frame, I'm walking to him, I stand right in front of him and all I can think is what a small mouth he has. Somehow I join his group and I'm going from place to place with his party, but I never get to talk to him. Then I'm in the big blue station wagon my daughter drives, but Hillary is driving. First she can't get the car started—I roll my eyes. Then we are lost. We are coming to the top of a hill, and she won't go over the crest because she's afraid the road doesn't continue and we will fall off.

Lorraine Evans, Accountant Turned Teddy Bear Artist
Age: 45
Ballwin, Missouri

On January 26, 1993, I wrote a letter to Hillary Rodham Clinton asking her to donate her inaugural hat for a fund-raising event, of which I was chairman.

I came into the lobby of my building, and the doorman gave me a package. He said, "It's from the White House, Mr. Fairchild." I said, "Thank you," and remained very calm, like this was a very normal thing. I got on the elevator to go up to my apartment and started tearing the box open on the elevator. I was about halfway up to my floor when I pulled back the tissue and saw the WRONG hat. It was a brown straw picture hat with a blue ribbon. On the remaining elevator ride, I thought, "How in the hell can I make this work? It's a sun hat, for Christ's sake!"

The elevator door opened and I went into my apartment, threw the box down, and swore at the Clintons. I picked up the antique phone in my foyer which calls the doorman, and when he answered, I told him to get the White House on the phone. He did and the phone began to ring. A voice answered, "Hello."

I said, "Hello, my name is Paul Fairchild and I would like to speak to whomever sent the wrong hat to me for the silent auction in Chicago."

The voice on the other end said, "Paul, this is Hillary, what do you mean they sent the wrong hat? I only have two!"

I said, "Well, they sent the straw picture hat, not the inaugural hat." Then the other line picked up and it was Bill.

"Paul, it's Bill. I can't believe they sent the wrong goddamn hat. Don't worry, we'll get you the right hat before the auction."

The foyer phone rang and the doorman told me President and Mrs. Clinton are here, may he send them up? I said yes, and the doorbell rang. I answered it and the Clintons came into my apartment. We went into the living room and Hillary opened her suitcase and gave me the inaugural hat. I thanked them and we started to chat about I don't know what and I awakened.

Paul Fairchild, Image Consultant
Age: 39
Chicago, Illinois

I was at a mobile home that belonged to a family friend and was used for weekend getaways. I came out of the master bathroom half dressed, and President Clinton was sitting on the bed in a suit and tie. He patted the spot next to him and said, "Sit down." As I did, Hillary and three Secret Service agents came in and Hillary said, "We have to go *now!*"

M. G., Wife and Mother
Age: 29
St. Louis, Missouri

I was copyediting a speech for President Clinton, under the extremely watchful eye of Hillary. She was very strong-willed, very domineering—while Bill Clinton didn't say a word and sort of stood off to the side. I remember thinking, "Now I understand why this man would have an affair!" Another strange thing about my copyediting is that the speech was already published in a bound book, and I kept referring to it to fix up what I was working on.

After a segment in which my art director and I were running away from an ex-boyfriend of mine around New York City's Madison Square Garden, I went over to Penn Station to sit on the steps that lead to the Long Island Railroad (Thirty-Second Street and Seventh Avenue). There were lots of other people there, all dressed to the nines, waiting for the President to make his speech. And that address was to be held during a variety show televised on CBS! First, a couple of awards were given out for animated short cartoons. Then, President Clinton walked out to the podium—and the dream ended.

D. L. (Female), Writer/Editor
Age: 36
Melville, New York

Everything was in Technicolor and silence. Hillary was part of a string quartet. The members were seated in a row on a stage that resembled the type found in high school auditoriums.

The quartet consisted of three faceless members playing two violins and a cello, and Hillary, who played a dulcimer held in her lap. She was wearing the blue outfit worn at the inauguration sans the hat, and her long hair was up in a French twist. She smiled contentedly as she looked down at and strummed the instrument. Bill quietly walked up behind her and placed his hands on her shoulders. He was dressed in a very plain gray suit with a red-and-white-striped tie. He also smiled contentedly as she continued to play, her attention fixed on her dulcimer.

L. S. T. (Female), Health Care Professional
Age: 45
Florence, South Carolina

Hillary was visiting Boulder, and in keeping with the community as a whole, it was to be a very casual visit. There was a very small reception for her in a small, not very impressive conference room. Only a handful of people were present, but she only wanted to speak with me. Specifically, she wanted to know what radio station to listen to while visiting. I told her the community radio station—a diverse alternative station which I support. She was impressed by the information I gave her on the station and said she would listen to it.

Then, in the manner of dreams, Bill was there getting his hair cut by just an ordinary barber. He wanted to get my opinion on his cut, so I ran my fingers through his hair to see what was possible. I was surprised to discover that his hair was quite fine (like mine), not the coarse, thick, wiry stuff I presumed it to be.

Then he vaporized, or became no longer important, and I was again talking with Hillary. She had recalled that she was next to visit Urbana, Illinois, and wanted to know what to listen to there. I told her about a community, alternative radio station in Urbana, and she thanked me for the information. Right after that she was gone.

Kate Greenberg
Age: NA
Boulder, Colorado

I Protect the President

I had three dreams of Bill while traveling in Nepal.

I was on the ground floor of a building in which Clinton was giving a speech. A guy that I knew from college ran past me with a loaf of bread and headed up the stairs. Somehow, I knew that the bread was actually a bomb. I ran up after him and I guess I diffused the bread, because it didn't explode. I don't clearly remember the rest of the details, but I think I met Clinton and he thanked me for saving his life, or maybe some Secret Service people came in and thanked me.

In another dream, Clinton was holding a question-and-answer session at my old university. I was the person assigned to greet him and escort him to the meeting room. I sat in the room and participated in the discussion, and then I think that I escorted him to a lunch with some other students, because I remember sitting next to him and talking to him at a table.

In another dream (I had about one a week in November, then it slowed down to one every two or three weeks, and now they seem to have stopped), I saved Chelsea from some kidnappers or terrorists or something. I don't remember the details, but Bill and Hillary were very grateful. I went to their house for dinner. I remember sitting at a counter with Clinton in a warm, suburban-style kitchen. We were both talking with Hillary as she stirred something on the stove.

Anne S. "Penny" Penniston, Unemployed Copywriter/
Recent College Graduate
Age: 23
Chicago, Illinois

While moving from the Arkansas Governor's Mansion to the White House, Clinton remarked on TV that he felt homeless, since he didn't have a home in the transition period. At the same time, I was contemplating a move from one small apartment to another one.

Later I dreamed that I contacted him and asked him to move in with me to share me and the rent—and he did! We lived happily ever after in a two-bedroom apartment in this small town, and I was the envy of the neighborhood. Hillary and Chelsea were not in the picture, thank goodness!

In my opinion he is a prime example of a "macho" man, and I like what he does with his hands! I'm seventy-four and retired—but I can dream, can't I???

Abbie Roush, Retired
Age: 74
Forest Grove, Oregon

January 14, 1993: I am President Clinton's bodyguard. I am deciding about clothes to wear for the evening's assignment.

January 17, 1993: On the upper floor of a large warehouse, President Clinton is engaged in a fight with guns with another man. Their guns are pointed barrel to barrel.

March 10, 1993: Again I am his bodyguard. President Clinton personally picks me to be responsible for his safety. He has absolute trust in me to protect him.

Marcena Zellers, Researcher for Information Services Company
Age: 37
Byron, Illinois

I dreamt he gave me his driver's license and told me to pretend to be him and fly somewhere. A lady at a desk said I wasn't Bill Clinton and shooed me away. I ran back to catch him, but he'd already gone beyond where I could go. I yelled, "Bill, it didn't work!" But he was gone. I cracked up upon waking.

James Coung, Artist/Student
Age: 26
Seattle, Washington

I was riding a horse on my daughter's ranch when I saw a man walking down the road toward me. As I rode up close to him I discovered it was Bill Clinton. He told me he had car trouble and wanted to use a telephone to call a garage for a tow truck. He climbed up on the back of the saddle, and I took him to the house, where he called for a tow truck. While we were waiting for the tow truck, he drank coffee and ate doughnuts. Bill showed me a cut on his finger that was caused when he tried to lift the hood of the car. I cleaned the wound and put a Band-Aid on his finger and I noticed his hands. They were strong and capable hands.

Then we got on the horse and I took him back to where his car was sitting at the side of the road. When he left with the tow truck driver, he thanked me and told me if I ever came to Washington, to be sure and come to the White House to visit. He told me I reminded him of his mother.

L.M.A. (Female), Retired Nurse
Age: 74
Aurora, Colorado

This took place in a town much like Kirksville. I was walking toward the downtown square when I noticed that Bill Clinton was being escorted to a podium to give a speech. I didn't know he was going to be there, and it appeared nobody else did either, because there wasn't a very large crowd.

The next thing I knew, I was in a stairwell, where I passed a very tall woman who mumbled that she was going to kill the President. I didn't pay any attention. As I was walking down the stairs, I was digging in my purse for a pen and something to write on. I finally got outside and reached Clinton just as he was leaving the podium. I began to ask him questions, scribbling his responses down on a bank deposit slip, and all the while he was walking toward an alley between two buildings.

As we walked I looked up just in time to see a door open on our left, and the woman I had seen earlier came out with a gun.

I grabbed her and held her against the door, and Clinton took the gun away from her. Then, as happens in so many dreams, she just disappeared.

The next thing I knew, Bill and Hillary and I were walking toward a small cabin in the woods nearby, and Bill was telling me they'd like to take me to dinner since I saved his life. We all changed clothes and went out. We were out among a crowd of people, and everyone was saying hello to Bill as if they'd known him all their lives. The attention he got was overwhelming, but he seemed to take it all in stride—for a while. Then it was like he just wanted to hide from it all. He put on this weird mask and started acting really silly, laughing and joking, and all I could think was, "Boy, this is the weirdest night of my life."

Amanda Thompson, Reporter
Age: 27
Kirksville, Missouri

I dreamed that my friend Amie ran out of a crowd of people to greet Bill while he was walking down a red carpet (kind of like the grand entrance the Hollywood stars make to the Academy Awards).

She had been drinking in this dream, and my part was saving her from making a fool out of herself. Bill responded by giving us a smile and that laugh of his.

Jennifer Ann Hopson, Recent College Grad Seeking Employment
Age: 22
Sunset Hills, Missouri

Invited to the White House

I was Bill Clinton's guest at the White House, and the President talked to me in a warm, folksy manner, as he would to a new friend. He told me stories of his growing up and being governor of Arkansas, and seemed genuinely interested in me. I felt quite comfortable with him, not nervous at all. It was entirely platonic; in fact, I met his wife. Hillary was at the sink in the kitchen, washing dishes herself. In the evening, Bill took me for a ride in Air Force One, and we flew low over Washington, D.C., as he pointed out the sights to me.

Kathleen F. Louden, Public Relations Manager
Age: 33
Evanston, Illinois

The President sat at the head of a long conference table made of a rich, heavy wood, and I sat at his right hand. There were beautiful books lining the walls. A few women and several men were working on an important assignment. I realized there were seven of us, and it all seemed very natural. Bill thanked us for completing the project, as he understood that it had been a tough assignment. I was feeling proud and relieved that the task had been completed. Everyone had worked relaxed—not at all uptight.

As other members of the team stood up I suddenly became self-conscious, and aware that I had been working with the President of the United States. I just went into a panic, knowing that I would never be that close to him again. I thought, "I must get his autograph at least twice for my grandchildren." Everybody who was on the "work team" was scrambling to touch the President. I couldn't find pencil and paper. I was being squeezed out of my place as I awoke from the dream.

Rebecca C. Black, Retired Social Worker
Age: 62
Charlotte, North Carolina

My wife, Debbie, and I were sitting in the White House eating dinner with Bill and Hillary Clinton. I was sitting across from the President, and Debbie sat across from Hillary. The table was set with *beautiful* china and crystal and goldware. There was a big gold candelabra on the table, a huge chandelier overhead, and beautiful formal drapes behind Bill.

We were eating and chitchatting, and servants were waiting on us. Debbie was on my right. Seated on my left was President Clinton's mother. The gentleman serving the table asked Debbie and me to pass President Clinton's mother her plate. As we passed it to our left, I noticed that it was an old metal (tin) pie plate with some old beat-up silverware (knife, spoon, and fork) thrown in it. As I laid it in front of the President's mother, the servant whispered in my ear, "She says *she* is from *Arkansas* and she doesn't like all this fancy eatin' stuff. This is all she'll eat out of."

President Clinton and Hillary looked at Debbie and me—at our shocked faces—and just threw back their heads and laughed.

Michael Curry, Nazarene Minister
Age: 42
Victoria, Texas

Before the inauguration, I dreamed that the Clintons had invited me to the White House because they had heard how interesting I was. First, Mrs. Clinton and I had a ninety-minute chat about, of course, me. Then, I stood in line with a group of common Americans waiting to meet Bill, the President.

After briefly shaking their hands, he saw me and motioned us to the couch and he said, in his Arkansas drawl, "So, you're Celia Sack! I've heard so much about you!"

Celia Sack, Rare Book Cataloguer
Age: 23
San Francisco, California

I was with an old girlfriend, who'd gone off the deep end and hasn't been seen or heard from since. She and I were spending a long weekend with the Clintons, probably in Hot Springs.

Bill had lost weight. He was in a wild party mood and running around in shorts and tank top. We were on a marina/home setting, probably at Lake Hamilton. We were all just real cozy, hangin' out, puttering around having a real extemporaneous, good time.

Then out of the water pops this huge snapping turtle with a really snide, slightly callous sense of humor. He looked at me and started singing this song to get my attention. It was kind of silly, but he was trying to tell me something, like the dreams you might have, when an owl is talking to you and then you wake, and forget everything, only to hear an owl hoot and fly away.

Lex Nuss, Corporate Security
Age: 40
Little Rock, Arkansas

I was going to the White House for a tour, similar to the one they had shortly after Inauguration Day. I was in a dress and heels, which I rarely wear. Chelsea took a few of us to the White House basketball court (I don't know if one really exists), and gave us a ball. I love basketball, and though the others seemed shy, I began to shoot. I went for a rebound and was dribbling the ball back toward the free throw line when all of a sudden Bill Clinton was guarding me. He was in yellow jogging shorts and a green T-shirt. I kept getting by him and making good shots, and I was amazed at how bad a basketball player he was. But he kept up with me, kept pushing me to play. I don't think he uttered a word, other than the usual basketball conversation.

J.D. (Female), Consultant/Attorney
Age: 35
Arlington Heights, Illinois

President Clinton was dressed in a navy blue suit, white shirt, and red tie. He and I were casually walking throughout the White House gardens. Everything was blooming and fragrant.

I was telling him in great depth about crime in our inner cities as well as the suburban areas. I explained many issues associated with gangs and what communities would have to do in order to stop their growth.

Throughout my dream, he appeared to be enthralled with every word I spoke. He seemed totally committed to fighting crime.

The strangest thing was, the next morning I saw him on television and I felt as if I had honestly had this conversation with him.

Barbara A. Gooderham, Director of Anticrime Organization
Age: 27
Pittsburgh, Pennsylvania

Both my husband and I were attending a conference with the President and Hillary. Everyone was sitting around a big table having coffee. There was a sense of excitement about being able to participate in the conference. We were each going to contribute information. Bill was friendly to everyone. Names were being checked on a list. They couldn't find my name. I said that I had received information in the mail and was definitely invited, but Clinton kindly and firmly said I had to leave. Hillary was sympathetic, and said I could stay and sit in on the meetings, but Bill said no. I was extremely disappointed.

I woke up feeling really sad, because I really wanted to participate and know what was being discussed. I also wanted to give my own input.

Donna Rahman, Mother/Housewife
Age: 39
San Jose, California

I was in bed with Bill Clinton. We were both simply lying there, quite content, having a pleasant conversation. This was not a "sexy" scene; however, I believe we were naked and covered with a sheet or blanket. At one point, a gentleman walked in and asked Bill a question. They continued to talk a while. The fact that someone walked in did not bother me at all, nor did the fact that they talked for a while. I was very content just being there with him. My response was, "Bill, don't you ever stop working?" This is all I remember. I was sorry to wake up, since it was such a pleasant dream.

J.G. (Female)
Age and Occupation: NA
Chicago, Illinois

In my dream, I woke up coughing late at night, and I was in a strange bed: a high, large, Queen Anne–style, four-poster bed. It was a very ornate room, and the clock said 2:30 A.M. I turned to my right and there was a woman lying next to me that I had never seen before, and lying next to her was a man reading with an Itty Bitty Book Light. I got out of bed and went over to his side, and was shocked to see it was Bill Clinton!

I said, "Oh, I'm so sorry, I hope my coughing didn't wake you."

He replied, "It's no problem, I'm always awake reading at this time."

I said, "What are you and I doing here, and who is that woman?"

He said, "Oh, this is part of my Getting to Know America Plan. I am going to sleep with two different people each night of my presidency."

With that I congratulated him on his victory, and then I left what turned out to be the Lincoln Bedroom.

J.A. (Female), Nurse/Anesthesia
Age: 36
Lincolnshire, Illinois

I received a message that Bill and Hillary wanted me at the White House to help them with something. I went straightaway with the sense of an urgent mission. When I got there, I was retained in a waiting room/parlor with a lot of hubbub and newspeople running around. I wondered what they had in store for me. When I finally saw them come in, they were preoccupied, rushing about, trying to get something set up, as if for a news conference. I watched the situation, trying to surmise the purpose of their calling for me. Gradually, I began to get a handle on the situation, and this time, instead of waiting for their instructions, I piped up with my own ideas. This caught their attention and it seemed as if my mission had become clear.

Marnie Glaser, School Psychologist
Age: 43
Chicago, Illinois

I dreamt I was living in the White House with Bill Clinton. I remember the interior of the house was dark brown wood.

I was showing my friends around the White House, and I remember saying we had to be quiet because Bill was working.

Lisa R. Tatge, College Student
Age: 28
Madison, Wisconsin

A few months ago, I dreamed that Hillary was serving me apple pie and coffee at the White House. She couldn't get the first slice out of the pan, so she called Bill in for help. He came in, served up the pie cheerfully and efficiently, and left. Hillary then complimented me on the scarf I was wearing. I told her it was a gift from one of my daughters (which it really was) and chose the opportunity to say, "By the way, both of my daughters are out of work" (which they really are). Hillary replied, "Well, I'll have to hold hearings about that!"

When I woke up, I had a feeling of satisfaction that I had conveyed my message to her and she would do something about it. Alas, the daughters are still out of work, so I guess she hasn't gotten around to it yet.

Dolores Morning, Retired Librarian
Age: 64
Elgin, Illinois

I am the White House chiropractor. Bill is not too keen on chiropractors in my dream. The bulk of the dream is Hillary giving my secretary (who is also my stepsister) a complete physical exam. She is explaining how she wishes exams to be conducted. Now for the funny part, visualize my secretary/sister standing naked, with Hillary and myself working on her while Bill stands in the doorway watching very intently. Not into chiropractic but loves to watch physicals.

Kern Taylor, D.C., CCSP, Chiropractor
Age: 32
Montara, California

I dreamt that my friend Joyce and I were visiting the White House and heard that President Clinton needed a haircut but didn't have time to go for one. My friend Joyce offered to cut his hair, and I would see him with the barber cape on while she "ruined" his hair. She zigzagged all around, and while she was doing this, I ran to get Mrs. Clinton and tell her my friend had never cut hair before.

When I saw the finished product, I remember giving the President two hundred dollars and saying, "Please, don't let any one else do this to you again."

Monica Grienlee, Retired
Age: 65
Westland, Michigan

I was visiting him in the White House, and late at night (around three A.M.), a knock came on my door as I was doing some reading. I got up and opened it, and the President was standing there barefoot in a pair of striped pajamas, hair tousled.

He asked if he could come in and talk with me about the letter I'd written him regarding my inability to find work. I was surprised that he would come to talk at this time of night, but you can't turn down the President, you know? We talked for the better part of an hour. When he left, he kissed me on the cheek and said to let him know if I ever needed a job and he would see to it that I got one. . .and I did. A government job!

Debra Wimer, Self-employed Writer
Age: 35
Escondido, California

I had been invited to the inauguration. It was a very glitzy affair with all the world's glitterati in attendance. It was also very formal, so instead of calling Bill "Bill," they called him William (as was indeed the case at the real do). They spoke of William Clinton, they spoke of that great American document, the William of Rights, and they also discussed at length the possi-william-ities for the next four years.

Jill Draper, Full-time Mom
Age: 36
University City, Missouri

I was visiting Bill and Hillary in the White House. They were treating me as a good friend. For some reason, we all (except Bill and Hillary) went outside and sat in a ring on the grass along with some other people. Then Bill came out, walked around the circle till he came to me. Then he bent down and removed my pants, and started performing oral sex on me. I liked it until, suddenly, Hillary came up. When I saw her, I jumped up and ran into a housing development. She jumped into a small green sports car and tried to catch me. Boy, she was angry! But I got away, and didn't go back.

Guerlain Boyd (Female), Owner, Gerry's Cleaning Service
Age: 57
Charlotte, North Carolina

i dreamed about bill clinton
   i met him a few days earlier at the avoca
   international
   airport. got to shake his hand.
   it was freezin. (not his hand—
   i mean the weather, this was in november.)

and in my dream, i went to this big party at
   the white house. owl lanterns everywhere.
   music, folding chairs in the lawn,
   paper napkins blowin in the wind. . .
   i go down these steps off to the side of the porch
   (i've never been to the white house before,
   i mean in my conscious state)
   but it looked kinda like an old southern mansion,
   wood, paint chipping here and there, railing loose,
   some weeds around the place, but nice.
   i remember thinking it felt nice to be there.

and so i go down and inside,
  and here it gets a little complex.
  low light, candle lit, very warm, and i'm walkin
  through all these arterial hallways, past folding
  tables, finger foods
  (i remember putting something in my mouth,
  something on a cracker, and i didn't like it,
  and i held it up against my palate until
  the coast was clear. weird.)

and i broke away from the party at one point,
  just to walk around in the white house, you know,
  and that's when i meet bill clinton.
  he's in a bathrobe, terry cloth, powder blue,
  closed,
  and he's as tall as i am,
  and tan, or wind burned, or just well lit,
  and he said, *"wanna see something neat?"*

and of course i do,
  and so we go through the labyrinth together, and i
  think he
  calls me by
  my name, and he raises a finger to his lips
  as we pass this huge room which had long glass
  panels as
  walls,
  you can see right in,
  and he says *"shhhhhhh. hillary."*
  and i look through the glass wall, and there
  she is, asleep on this big round bed,
  and then i had to catch up to him because
  he kept walkin. and we go deeper and deeper.

i see kids in bunk beds stayin over,
    clothes on the floor, toys, books, you know,
    everything is open, not a closed door in sight.
    and we approach this really narrow, dark
    corridor, wooden floor squeakin and all,
    and we turn the corner
    and there it is,
    all lit up, electric humming, big.
    (and i swear all this is exactly as i dreamed it)
    it was this really industrial looking,
    neon glowing buzzing vending machine.
    this huge vending machine,
    and bill bites over his lower lip with his upper
    teeth, and in a voice like a little kid on
    christmas morning, he said,
    "häagen-dazs, ben and jerry's. frozen yogurt too.
    and you don't have to put quarters in.
    what kind you want?"
    and i think i said chunky monkey
    because i like sayin those words together.
    i forget what flavor he got.
    but we stood in that little area
    in the humming of that vending machine,
    in the light of its electric buzz,
    both of us goin
    "mmmmmmm. mmmmmmm. mmmmmm..."

and that was the dream.
    that's it
    me and bill clinton eatin pints of ice cream
    all by ourselves in the white house,
    having a hi ho time.

one more thing about this dream.
when i retold the dream later on that day,
someone asked me two things.
what was she wearin,
and
did you vote for him.

pajamas and you bet i did.

Henry Long, Artist/Cook
Age: 31
Wilkes-Barre, Pennsylvania

My mother and I were having lunch with Bill in the White House kitchen. He was in casual dress, standing at the refrigerator door, which was wide open, asking us what we would like to eat, because he was going to make it.

Dawn Anderson, Loan Officer for a Credit Union
Age: 30
Longmont, Colorado

My dream took place before his election to the Presidency. I was visiting the Clinton family at the White House. It was Christmastime, and we were all involved in decorating the very large, very tall tree in the spacious living room. Chelsea and I went outside for a moment to look at the silent falling snow, and we looked in wonder at the beauty of the White House in the early winter evening.

Suzanne Pfleger
Age: 35
Buffalo, New York

A few days before the election, I dreamed my husband, Ewell, our daughter, Ashley (three years old), and myself were invited to the White House. Ashley was very excited about meeting Chelsea and Socks the cat. We all had a very casual dinner together. I remember feeling happy and at peace. Then President Clinton and First Lady Hillary Rodham Clinton showed us our room. It was a large room with a lot of sunshine coming through the windows. It had a large balcony, and when I walked out there with my daughter, it overlooked President Kennedy's grave, which we all know is not at the White House. President and First Lady Clinton joined us and we all held hands in total silence.

Patricia McAlexander Hunt, Retired Substance Abuse Counselor,
Now a Full-time Mom
Age: 42
Rocky Mount, Virginia

I was a top member of Clinton's transition team. He was introducing me to the other aides, and convening a meeting, when I looked down and realized I had forgotten to change out of my nightclothes. So, I attended my first transition meeting in a red and white flannel nursing gown. (I was nursing a baby at the time.)

R.W.C., Bank Branch Manager
Age: 38
Flint, Michigan

Jogging With the President

I was out taking my morning walk, but instead of walking as usual, I was jogging with Bill Clinton. I wasn't on our street as usual—I was on the sidewalk in a downtown city area. As we approached the traffic signal, President Clinton (who was wearing this ugly, flowered, multicolored shirt and knee-length green shorts, and had on a blue baseball cap, and was listening to his Walkman) stopped and walked along beside me. He put his arm up around my shoulder, and I returned the gesture and we walked along (as I used to in elementary school with my "best buddy") in a "best buddy ol' pal" way.

He then asked me to buy $200,000 of term life insurance from him. He said that he and Hillary weren't taking in near so much money since he'd become President as when he was governor of Arkansas, and so he had to sell insurance on the side to make up the difference. I told him I already had plenty of life insurance and really couldn't afford more coverage because we were on a tight budget ourselves. Then he said, "But couldn't you *drop* your coverage with your current agent and take out this coverage with me instead? I need the business!"

So I said, "Well, okay, if it will help you out."

Then we started across the street to a doughnut shop together, and President Clinton says to me, "I hate to go in public places to eat my doughnut and coffee, because as soon as I enter, people just crowd in around me, and it gets old after a while!"

So I said, "Well, come on over to our house. Debbie (my wife) will fix you some coffee and give you a doughnut." So we did, but when we walked in, it wasn't the house where I live now (nor any of the other four homes I've lived in lately). But it was our *first* little frame house we bought right after we got out of college back in Bethany, Oklahoma.

I took President Clinton into the little kitchen, which we had redecorated in typical early 1970s style in big, bright yellow-and-orange-and-green flowered wallpaper (which, by the way, matched the colors in this ugly shirt he had on). Deb didn't react in any way because I'd brought the President home. She had on her bathrobe, no makeup, and she hadn't combed her hair yet. She just said, "Sure, I'll fix you some coffee." She gave him a doughnut, which he stuffed into his mouth. I was thinking as I woke up, "Imagine the President of the United States having coffee and doughnuts in our little kitchen."

Michael Curry, Nazarene Minister
Age: 42
Victoria, Texas

Again I had a dream in which Bill Clinton was in a jogging outfit, but this time, so was I. There were Secret Service people and some other people, and we were all jogging. I think it was supposed to be Washington, D.C.—we were running through tunnels and buildings, and President Clinton was setting a wicked pace. I was determined to stay right behind him. I was gasping for air as we ran into a tunnel. My labored breathing was echoing loudly. He stopped, turned around and grabbed me, and said, "You can do it," and then started asking me about taxes.

J.D. (Female), Consultant/Attorney
Age: 35
Arlington Heights, Illinois

I approached Hillary, saying, "You don't know me, but you should, since when you were a freshman at Wellesley I was a senior" (which is true). We began talking as if we were old friends and were soon joined by Bill. We three started walking and talking—again completely comfortable, as if good friends—then we began jogging down the street.

The night before the above dream, my daughter, Rebecca, dreamed that I was talking nonsense to Bill, thus embarrassing her terribly.

Ann Thomas Wilkins, Ph.D., University Lecturer
Age: 49
Pittsburgh, Pennsylvania

I dreamt I was jogging with President Clinton on an icy winter day. At first, he was ahead, but I caught up with him and passed him. He was out of breath and having a difficult time jogging, but I was having an easy run, even though I was wearing uncomfortable black boots. A bunch of Secret Service agents were with Bill, and one came over to me and was chatting and jogging along with me. The entire entourage entered and exited each row house as we passed by, and folks were shouting, "It's Bill. It's Bill Clinton!"

Miriam Derman, Dance Movement Therapist
Age: 33
Evanston, Illinois

I was in Washington, D.C., at some public gathering where Clinton was. I asked him if he'd like to play racquetball (since it is a favorite sport of mine). He said he thought it would not be appropriate at that time. Later in the day, he was jogging and asked me if I'd like to join him. I said I'd love to. Shortly after we started he said, "Let's see if we can get rid of these Secret Service people!" So we were running across yards, jumping hedges and fences, and hiding in garages and outdoor sheds. It was fun!! He finally said he had to go, thanked me for the run, and left.

Arlen Ottmar, High School Band Director
Age: 43
Iowa City, Iowa

I'm in Washington, and I'm out jogging with the President. We're both in sweatsuits and loping along in a parklike setting, from which the various monuments of the city are visible. I'm thinking to myself how incredible it is that I'm doing this, and making mental notes to write to various friends about it. Then I realize Bill is talking to me, telling me a story, which I can actually remember! (You know how hard it is to recall the exact words from dreams.) The story had to do with Southern accents, and how you have to get them just right in order to convey the full flavor of Southern anecdotes. Then he told me that at construction sites in the South, they don't have signs that say Men Working. Instead, the signs say Look Out—Guys Sawing Things. But he pronounced the words more like "Gahs Sawwwin' Thangs." Even awake, I think that's funny.

Judith Anne Testa, University Professor
Age: 50
Chicago, Illinois

Just Plain Bill

In my first dream, I drove up to what appeared to be a huge garage behind the White House. The garage door opened and I pulled in. I got out of my car and President Clinton came up to me and introduced himself. We shook hands and I introduced myself. The most lasting impression I had after the dream was that I wasn't nervous or overly excited to be meeting the President. In fact, I felt as if I was talking to a "regular guy"—like someone I'd known all my life. We talked briefly about some projects I've been working on at the American Academy of Pediatrics and then I left.

In the second dream, I was at a White House function and President Clinton was there. There were a lot of people sitting around a huge circular table discussing various national issues. Only a select group of people were invited to meet the President after the discussion and there was a great sense of "who would be chosen." I was one of them and was ushered into another room. I went up to President Clinton to introduce myself, but before I could say my name, he said, "I know, you're Lisa Reisberg." Again, we got to talking about work-related projects, and this time, he told me he was very proud of the work I've been doing. Just then, Hillary came up next to me and took me by the hand (I also remember that she was holding my hand very tightly). She led me around the room, pointing out different items that for some reason were being exhibited. In this dream, I felt very secure about our country's future and was glad that our President was "just like everyone else."

Lisa Reisberg, Director of Public Education/
American Academy of Pediatrics
Age: 34
Schaumburg, Illinois

In my dream, I was on a bus with a lot of people. The bus was like the campaign bus, and everyone on it was laughing and talking and having a good time. I knew that President Clinton was on the bus before I saw him, but I was surprised when I finally saw him he was puffing on a big cigar! He was dressed casually, in a baseball jacket (like the one he wore when he threw out the ball in Baltimore). How could this be possible? Hadn't Hillary declared the White House a no-smoking zone? Ah, but Hillary wasn't on the bus; maybe Bill was catching a smoke while she wasn't around.

What to do? I am very allergic to smoke of any kind and especially cigar smoke. Obviously, I was going to have trouble if this was going to be a long trip. Was I going to suffer and have bronchial problems or ask the President to put out his cigar?

The next thing I knew, I was approaching Bill Clinton. He looked very friendly, quite a nice-looking man. I said hello and asked him if he would mind putting out the cigar. He was very pleasant and said, "Of course, I'm really glad you told me about this; I wouldn't want to cause you any discomfort."

I went back to my seat pleased at the outcome but just a little embarrassed and amazed at myself for having done what I did. Thinking what a nice man our President was.

Gloria Clark, Nurse/Cofounder of Support Group for Stepfamilies
Age: 62
Pittsburgh, Pennsylvania

Bill Clinton is leaning down where some men are digging a ditch. This is at night in a big city. Bill Clinton is in a nice suit, and he's on the ground, which is dirty and muddy. He gets up and he has dust on him. He laughs that he's trying to get dirty like an ordinary person. Al Gore is in the background and is wearing a short shirt and pants.

Nat Perkins, Jr., Telephone Interviewer/Apartment Shopper
Age: 37
Houston, Texas

I had just come out of the ladies' restroom at Mall 205. I saw President Clinton and some men all dressed in navy blue suits except for the President—he was wearing a beige suit. They were walking down the mall very fast and talking seriously. President Clinton looked absolutely handsome and smiling all the time.

Rose L. Bresnehan, Retired
Age: 71
Portland, Oregon

President Clinton was spending the night at my house. He got up in the middle of the night looking for the bathroom. I could only see his back. He had on boxer shorts with urine stains on them. I was very concerned, and I helped him to find the bathroom.

He was sleeping in a small bedroom with a wood floor. I was very concerned about finding a rug to put on the floor so he would be more comfortable.

Florence Jeter, Waitress
Age: 44
Lexington, Kentucky

I dreamed I was just getting ready to sit down on a sofa because I was tired, and I was kind of falling down, and Bill Clinton put his hand under my behind, and I was struggling to keep from sitting on it, and jumped like crazy in bed—so much that I woke up my husband, who had a good laugh when I told him what I was dreaming about.

Elsie M. Archer, Housewife
Age: 61
Pine Grove, Pennsylvania

An old girlfriend and I were walking through the parking lot of my high school. We were casually strolling along, headed in the direction of some sort of nightclub. I was wearing very tight black pants, a short, cropped shirt, and high heels. (I hadn't dressed or looked like that since my much thinner youth when I frequented clubs, before I met my husband and had two children.)

We were going to the club, when a small, pale green, two-door hatchback drove up and blocked our path. The driver, a bearded man in his thirties, looking burned-out and dazed, stared straight ahead as the passenger spoke. "Hey, would you girls care for a ride?" the sleepy-eyed Bill Clinton asked.

"No thanks," we replied.

"Okay man, that's cool," and they were off.

It is worth mentioning that Mr. Clinton seemed very attracted to me.

Valerie Railsback-Vogt, Art History Student
Age: 28
Houston, Texas

I am wandering around in a small town. Bill Clinton appears and asks me to take him clothes shopping. I am delighted and surprised that the President has asked me to take him shopping, but I realize I have good taste, so why not? I take him to Reyn's Clothing Store, which in the dream looks like a tacky touristy shop, not the establishment I am used to seeing. He pulls out a matching shirt and shorts set. I shake my head. . .like he could have made a better choice. We continue shopping.

L. Kuhns (Female), Fund-raiser
Age: NA
Honolulu, Hawaii

Lost Objects

Before I had this dream, my son died on Friday the 11th of December, 1992, at 11 o'clock on highway 22 (11+11) North in Jackson Hole, Wyoming, Teton County.

I dreamt Bill Clinton came to my shop in a white minivan. He parked just below the bay window that my barber pole is mounted in. Bill came into my shop with his daughter trailing behind him, her name was Chauncey, she was only about five or six years old. Bill wanted me to cut her hair. He placed her on the lift seat, he was very charismatic and gentle. It took quite a long time to cut her hair, she moved around a lot. In the process Bill asked me if there was any one thing, out of all the things we had discussed, that was troubling me. I told him that I was very concerned about North Korea. He said he was somewhat concerned, but not to worry, he had eleven people on his staff working on the problem.

Well, finally I finished Chauncey's haircut and walked Mr. Clinton to his minivan. When we got to his van, I picked Chauncey up and was holding her because a car was trying to come through the lot and get by the minivan. As I turned around to make sure we were out of the way the car backed up and pulled away. As the car was pulling away Mr. Clinton had another child in the minivan that I did not know about. As he picked the child up the child appeared to be a bunny rabbit, white and soft and furry. We said our goodbyes and Mr. Clinton said he would stop by and see me the next time he came through.

I went back into the shop. Some customers had entered when I was saying goodbye to Mr. Clinton. One customer I knew well, in fact he had recently asked about my son, who had died earlier that month in a car accident. I had just gotten ready to cut his hair when in came Bill. The customers who were waiting tried to act casual and calm upon seeing the President. It seemed that Bill had lost an oval-shaped object that his wife had given him and she would be very upset if he lost it. I have a small black church pew in my barber shop for my clients to sit on. I was half kneeling, half lying on the floor, searching for the object, as I had been on the day I received the news of my son's death, and there at my foot was an oval-shaped aquamarine stone. Aquamarine was my son's birthstone. Mr. Clinton was very pleased to have recovered the object, and we said goodbye again. He asked me to stop in and see him the next time I came to town, and he would certainly make it a point to stop in again to see me.

James C. Lane, Barber
Age: 46
Roanoke, Virginia

President Clinton was to visit our house. The presidential helicopter was flying across the field in back of our house. I remember I couldn't find my video camera. I was frantic that the

President was coming and I wouldn't be able to capture the moment on tape. I don't think I ever did find my camera, and my dream ended when the helicopter landed behind our house.

Frederick J. Mack, Pharmacist
Age: 38
Boulder, Colorado

Metamorphosis

I am at a party in a nice, but not fancy, suburban house. There's a medium-sized crowd, but still plenty of elbow room. The President arrives, and I know I want to chat with him. I find myself standing by the fireplace mantel with him as we sip our mineral water. I tell him that I really empathize with what he's been going through—the public scrutiny, the attempt to instigate change in the face of the blindness and lack of vision of the old guard, the feeling that people have put him on a pedestal and expect miracles, the ensuing blame when things don't change overnight (Americans are so immature!). I tell him that some of my empathy comes from the fact that I have been in a position where people have expected certain things from me, and when I haven't lived up to their expectations, I have suffered for it.

In his case, of course, the situation is far more stressful. All this time, he is listening very closely and in an interested manner. I feel like we are friends. There are no Secret Service people around or other people—just the two of us. Then I look closely at him and realize that he has the same build as he does normally, but that his face, while very tan, is extremely wrinkled due to the stress of the last five months. I also realize that his face is now that of Jimmy Carter!

Deborah S. Page, Elementary School Teacher
Age: 43
Mill Valley, California

I was at some sort of reception or informal party in a large hall, with many people in attendance. I was chatting with a few people when I noticed Bill Clinton nearby.

He saw us, too, and came over as if to speak with us, but he never said a word. He stood face-to-face with me in his suit and tie, hands at his sides. As he turned with his open palms toward me, he began to turn into light, until he was an outline of a man, filled with brilliant, dazzling light. I thought to myself, "Amazing! Our President is a being of light!" I was so stunned that I woke up feeling blessed and happy, and as if I had been let in on a wonderful secret.

Dilsha Anne Carpenter Happel, Educational Consultant/
Resource Person to Parents with Special Needs
Age: 42
Boulder, Colorado

The dream began in an Indian restaurant somewhere in Japan. President Clinton was there to make a speech and was talking with me prior to this taking place. I had my back to him and he was holding me and kissing my neck. This was somewhat sexual but mostly friendly.

He went on into the side room prior to making his entrance for the speech. Hillary and I were talking then and I introduced her to many friends. One of my best friends was particularly impressed by her. I then introduced her to many Japanese and I was amazed that she was able to converse in common Japanese.

Hillary went into the room where the speech was to be presented. I had to go to the bathroom. As I was leaving the bathroom to hear the speech, I looked in the mirror and noticed that I had a terribly large knot on the top of my forehead. It looked fuzzy and strange. I began to flake it with my finger and out came beautiful rubies. I was amazed and showed some of the rubies to some Middle Easterners. At this point, the restaurant was Middle Eastern. We were all fascinated as the rubies changed color from bright red to more of the real ruby color of pigeon's blood. I remember thinking as they were turning, "I hope these are real."

Karen Crandall, International Designer
Age: NA
Sugar Land, Texas

I witnessed some Republicans hoisting a tall, solid statue of Bush/Reagan, and right below the statue was a small snowman-like statue of Clinton/Carter that was melting. I remember being annoyed at the Republicans for again thinking that they were strong and right and that Clinton was a lightweight, until I realized that as the snowman statue of Clinton/Carter was melting, an effervescent, sparkly, powerful, angeliclike energy was inside beneath the melting facade.

Bill Wing, Psychotherapist
Age: 39
St. Louis, Missouri

My Dad Bill

I am sitting, having lunch with Hillary. Suddenly, Bill walks up wearing a short-sleeved shirt. Bill sticks out his hand and says, "I really like your work." And I say, "It's me who should be saying I'm impressed with you." Bill puts his arm around my shoulder, and we stroll off to a baseball park and watch the game. Later, we are sitting in the stands together. This was an extremely comforting dream. It felt like I was with a guru or a deceased father. I woke up feeling great, relaxed.

Alan Sacks, Producer
Age: 50
Hollywood, California

Bill was my father and the Clintons and I were at the inauguration (which was in what seemed to be a high school gymnasium or cafeteria or something similar). Bill (Dad) was about to give his speech, and Hillary, Chelsea, and I were taking our seats—I sat between them. Hillary and I were discussing our clothes. I felt like I wasn't dressed up enough, but Hillary assured me that I looked fine. She said that this was a young administration and they just wanted everyone to feel comfortable and to be casual. I felt like she was trying to get on my good side because she wanted us to get along for Dad's sake. Chelsea pretty much ignored me and I assumed she was feeling a little jealous. Dad finished his speech and came to sit with us. He asked how I liked being there, and I told him I thought things would be a little more formal, and then he said basically the same thing Hillary had told me earlier about wanting things to be casual, which I thought was cool. Then I started thinking about whether or not I should live in the White House. First I thought it would upset my mom, but then I starting thinking it would be pretty cool to live there with all the maids and the chef and the private screening room. I thought it would be fun to have my friends over. I decided I would just visit a lot. While I was thinking about this, Al Gore got up to give his speech, and he didn't have a shirt on. I was a little taken aback, so I asked Dad about it, and he just laughed it off and said that they just wanted everyone to have a good time and enjoy themselves today.

My most vivid memory of this dream (besides the fact that Al Gore had an incredible chest) was the feeling that Bill was really my father and it was common knowledge to everyone. It just felt like a family function—sort of like a company picnic, only a little more important.

A.S. (Female), Student
Age: 22
Sherman Oaks, California

I'm in a beautiful bedroom, looking through a closet full of nice clothes. I am trying to decide what to wear to the presidential inauguration. It then dawns on me that I am the daughter of Bill Clinton and that I am going to be on national television! In the dream, I am myself, not Chelsea Clinton, but I am still the President's daughter. I decide to wear one of my favorite dresses, which is backless and quite revealing. I start to laugh because I know if I wear this dress, the tattoo on my left shoulder will be broadcast on national television and the press will have a field day talking about the President's tattooed daughter.

The next thing I know, I am standing in the White House Rose Garden surrounded by reporters. Each is shouting my name and asking me questions about my father, President Clinton. Then Bill Clinton sticks his head out of one of the White House windows and yells at me to stop playing with the reporters and to come inside and get ready for the inauguration.

Next, I am running upstairs in the White House. I run down this hallway where there are a bunch of apartments. There are shots fired in one of the apartments, and the next thing I know, Secret Service men are swarming into this apartment. A woman I don't know has been shot dead. Inside the apartment are all kinds of guns, ammunition, and materials to make bombs. I think to myself that this is strange and will probably put a damper on the inauguration.

Laurie L. Chapé, Communications Director
for a Credit Union League
Age: 32
Aiea, Hawaii

My Pal Bill

A few nights after the election, I dreamt Bill and I were sitting around in a living room and I was congratulating him on the win. The tone was such that he was obviously a good friend of mine, and the whole setting was very informal. The one outstanding feature was the background music. It was something like Steely Dan and I remember thinking, "Wow! The President and I like the same music—this is a first!"

S.S.M. (Female), Research Scientist Turned Homemaker
Age: 35
Pittsburgh, Pennsylvania

Dream 1

Bill and I were kidnapped separately and brought to the same hideaway, located somewhere in the Middle East.

We were put in a room together and had a lot of time on our hands to get to know each other. After what seemed like days of conversation, bewildered, I asked Bill, "With severe allergies, how do you accomplish all that you do?" Simply and directly, Bill responded, "I choose not to focus on them."

The next day, I awoke with a new attitude toward having disabling allergies and chemical sensitivities. Truly I was inspired to rehabilitate myself.

Dream 2

Bill was the teacher in an adult education class I was attending in an effort to rehabilitate myself. Being oversensitive to heat as well as fragrances and other chemicals, I was overwhelmed by the heat in the classroom. Bill reassigned my seat to sit beside a man in a three-piece business suit who was wearing cologne. This seat assignment didn't improve my situation. Still I was completely overwhelmed and near fainting.

Bill looked at his seat-assignment chart and told me not to worry—that he would find a safe place for me.

Dream 3

After Bill's first bombing of Iraq, reporters surrounded the President while he was taking time off to visit with friends that included me.

After a few moments of reporters intensely interrogating and hurling accusations of being a warmonger, Bill began crying convulsively. I took him aside and told him to talk to me, that he could trust me.

As he continued to sob he managed to tell me, "I didn't become President to kill anyone. I didn't want to do it! I want to quit. I only want to help people, not kill innocent citizens."

I held the president in my arms, comforting him as he sobbed on my shoulder.

Maya Cynthia Fisher, Unemployed Due to Disability
From Multiple Chemical Sensitivities and Allergies
Age: 36
Boulder, Colorado

My husband and I lived next door to the Clintons (or he lived next door to us—I can't remember if he lived in our neighborhood or we lived in Arkansas). They were leaving to move to Washington. We had a heartfelt goodbye. We were very good friends. During the dream, I had an overwhelming good feeling of warmth and friendship. We were all sad to be parting, and Bill assured us we'd remain friends and he'd visit often. It seemed we often went to him for advice, and he was always available and willing to talk, and genuinely concerned. Apparently, we knew him a long time. For a long while after I woke up, I felt deeply saddened that it was only a dream. I still felt overwhelmed. I thought it was a bit odd to feel such strong emotions during and after a dream.

Lori Malinski, Professional Fund-raiser
Age: 32
Chicago, Illinois

I live alone and have a little terrier dog named Possum. In my dream, I had lost Possum and was out on the highway looking for him. This large black car stopped, and President Bill Clinton peered out the back window and asked me if I had any kind of trouble, and if I needed a ride.

He noticed that I was upset, and asked if he could help me in any way. I explained about my dog. He said, "We will help you look for Possum." His staff left the limousine and looked for the dog.

We started talking; he was still in the car. We talked health care for the elderly, and child care for single parents. We shared our views on several subjects, and I told him, the only thing I had ever thought about Arkansas was that we that call it home find it hard to live anywhere else.

About this time, my little dog came running up to the car. Bill opened the door and Possum and Bill got to be friends fast. I apologized for the dog jumping in the seat. He said, "Don't you worry one bit about it." Then I noticed the dog hair on his navy blue suit. As I tried my best to get all of it off his coat, I woke up. The next day he was on the TV in a news conference wearing the same navy blue suit and red striped tie he wore in my dream.

Georgia Babbitt, Health Care Worker
Age: 59
Bryant, Arkansas

I guess it was about a day after Clinton was elected. In the dream, I was at my parents' house in Westchester. My mother and father were there, and we were eating lunch. Bill drove up in the driveway in this '83 Cutlass, and we went for a drive. He was wearing a polo shirt and jeans, and we just cruised around the neighborhood. He was quite normal except that he had trouble looking me in the eye. He seemed preoccupied. I said to him, "I'm really glad you're going to be our President." He smiled and said, "Thanks." He almost needed a shave. It was a very warm, friendly dream, as if everything was all right and was going to stay all right from now on.

J.M. (Male), Housepainter/Rock Singer/Songwriter
Age: 30
New York, New York

I was leaving my house to run a few errands. It was late on a Saturday afternoon. It was very pleasant outside. Bill came strolling down my street and asked me if my name was Kathy Lightfoot. I answered in the affirmative, a bit awestruck I might add. He said he had the afternoon free and was wondering if he could hang with me for the afternoon. I told him I would be delighted to have the company.

Bill accompanied me on my errands. We first filled the car up with unleaded—he pumped the gas. Then we made a quick trip to the grocery store to pick up a few items for a new barbecue recipe I wanted to try that night. After a quick run to the drive-through at the bank, we returned to my home. As Bill fired up the grill outside, I began to prepare dinner in the kitchen. I soon heard him talking to someone. My husband had arrived home early from work, and they were shooting the breeze at our picnic table.

When I brought out a few appetizers, my husband took the drink orders. We were all in deep conversation regarding neighborhoods, soaring property taxes, the crime rate, and the question of whether we should have our new female puppy spayed or not.

It was great sharing the afternoon and early evening with our new friend. He said he would return for another barbecue for my mom's birthday in July so he could meet the rest of the family. That's it—my alarm brought me back to reality.

Oh yeah, Bill drinks Scotch on the rocks, no twist.

Kathleen Lightfoot, Legal Secretary
Age: 38
River Forest, Illinois

In the fall of '92, I dreamed I was with the Clinton family, who were relaxing in a house with large, airy rooms and lots of sunlight. Chelsea and I were hanging out, took a walk around outside, and hit it off. Then Bill at the far left of a table, Hillary in the middle, and Chelsea at her left were discussing a trip with me.

Chelsea asked if I would go to California with them. I said, "Probably."

Bill asked, "What can you do for us?"

I said, "I can help you with your diet."

Lex Nuss, Corporate Security
Age: 40
Little Rock, Arkansas

I was home with my four-year-old son, Andrew. We were getting ready to clean up the house and do the dishes. I looked out the front window, and a limousine unexpectedly pulled up. The next thing I see, Bill Clinton and Al Gore are walking up to the front door. I invited them in and apologized for the mess.

Then Bill said, "Don't worry about it. I'll have Al Gore clean it up and do the dishes. He can also watch Andrew while we take a ride in your car."

I have a 1976 Buick Skylark that is a little bit rusty on the back and has been welded a couple of times to hold the right front wheel axle together so it doesn't fall apart. Bill wanted to drive the car, so I let him. I sat on the passenger side, and two Secret Service agents sat in the back.

I live in Florida but we ended up driving in Connecticut, where I used to live. Bill was driving toward the University of Connecticut.

He was driving pretty fast. I was trying to tell him not to go so fast because the car might fall apart. Then we pulled up to my father's old house in Connecticut. As we were walking to the door, I noticed Al Gore was finishing washing the windows of the house. As we walked inside the house, I noticed a couple of Secret Service agents crouched down on one knee, holding machine guns as they slept in this position. Then I asked Bill, "Why don't they just go upstairs to the bedroom and sleep?" He responded, "That's how they sleep when they are watching me."

Peter Bobrek, Unemployed
Age: 42
Bradenton, Florida

I dream about him all the time. My favorite pre-election dream was when Bush was refusing to debate. Since I worked for the Clinton campaign as a volunteer, my dream took place at headquarters.

I was walking down the hall and could see "Bill" seated at a table in a room at the end. I was grousing at high volume about what a chicken Bush was, "What's he afraid of?" etc., and Bill was trying to shush me. I walked into the room and there was George Bush (they were negotiating when to debate). I felt so silly.

In all of my dreams, Bill and Hillary are my "pals." After the election, I dreamed Hillary asked me to help her decorate the White House! I have absolutely no talent in that regard and was in a total panic about how to decorate the White House. How about a nice, scrubbable vinyl wallcovering in the Blue Room?

Jan Caughey, Sales Representative for Wallcovering Distributor
Age: 41
Rockville, Maryland

I went to visit my friends Pat and Cari. They have a large wooded backyard, and as I enter it, I see a man with his back to me, talking to some other friends. When he turns around, I see it's Bill Clinton. I'm overjoyed to have this opportunity to get to speak with him, and find him very affable and communicative. We all share some good laughs, and when it's time for me to leave, I tell Bill some of my ideas for improving the country. He is very interested and I can tell he cares and is listening.

Katy Grischy, Psychotherapist
Age: 45
San Jose, California

I dreamt that I was walking around the yard with Bill Clinton. He was drinking something out of a metal shot "glass," and we were conversing about the problems of the day. He seemed to appreciate my insights and wanted to talk more. I was feeling like there was enough of a rapport for me to bring up the topic of abortion (the reason I did not vote for him), and I was awakened by one of my kids.

D.S.K., Housewife
Age: 35
Kingston, Rhode Island

A seventy-eight-year-old friend of mine named John is in jail for some unknown reason. When Bill Clinton happens to come to town and finds out John is in jail, he not only has him released immediately but invites him as his guest for dinner.

Bill Wing, Psychotherapist
Age: 39
St. Louis, Missouri

Mayor Freeman Bosley, Jr. (the first black mayor of St. Louis), Comptroller Vivus Jones, and President Clinton were riding around St. Louis in a limo. President Clinton was in the middle.

Strange thing was that I was in the back. Each one turned around and looked at me. They all had smiles on their faces. I had this warm feeling that I belonged with them in politics.

Jacqueline Parker, Phlebotomist
Age: 49
St. Louis, Missouri

Nightmares

I have had two dreams of Bill Clinton. The first was before the election, the second, after. Here they are in order of occurrence:

Bill Clinton was in a terrible flood, and somehow I was on dry ground observing him. His head was going under the rushing water, and yet he managed to pull himself above water by grabbing on to a floating billboard. He was having trouble grabbing on, and it was then that I noticed that his fingers were cut off! But he made it!

Another time, I dreamed that Bill Clinton was in a wheelchair and I asked him, "Can you get by here, Mr. President?"

"Hell, yes," he replied. I don't remember the ensuing dream conversation, but I do remember that I made him laugh.

David Allison, Actor
Age: 30
San Jose, California

I was journeying by train over the space of three or four days. Upon my return, someone referred in passing to the death of Bill Clinton by food poisoning, which, from the sound of it, had occurred soon after my departure. I found it hard to believe that such an important event would not have been made known to me through some means during the trip. Incredulous, I looked to a television hanging in the room where I stood, probably part of a restaurant.

Sure enough, Al and Tipper Gore had center stage in an event that was being televised at that very moment. They were having a White House ceremony to honor Hillary Clinton, who looked haggard and crippled, confined to a wheelchair. She had obviously been devastated by Bill's death—her hair had turned white. The ceremony had a banal and sentimental air—they treated her like a kind of poster child, condescendingly making naive jokes with her. I was reminded of several of Jim Brady's visits to the White House following the 1981 shooting. The Gores appeared to have taken over the reins of power rather commandingly and self-confidently. The death of Bill Clinton did not seem recent and traumatic, but seemed to belong to an immemorial, mythical past. Those around me seemed to have accepted it long ago. I alone was left to grieve in my shock.

Graham Harman, Graduate Student, Philosophy
Age: 24
Mt. Vernon, Iowa

I was the Clintons' maid in a hotel somewhere in Washington. Bill was lying without a shirt on, on a large rumpled bed.

I could not look at him as he spoke to me, because he looked superhuman, or sometimes extraterrestrial, depending on the moment I glanced at him.

He was magnetic. He was flirting with me. I tried to maintain a businesslike tone of interest in our discussion. His voice rose with idealistic platitudes, the hopes and dreams pouring out. He spoke in terms that I wanted to hear. I was afraid to look at him because I was afraid my will, perhaps my very soul, would be sucked out of me. A lot of dream time was spent in this heart-pounding internal struggle.

I was arranging things on the bureau and shelves when I saw the stash of pot. Pot littered the foot of the bed. Half-smoked joints had been rubbed out on the floor. . .a grubby lighter. . .a pipe. I decided not to react. I decided to move into the bathroom. The farther away from Bill, the more self-control I thought I could muster.

I opened the bathroom door and there was Hillary, doing a mudpack in the tub. Hillary, lying naked, bare breasts and legs entirely covered in half-dried mud. Thin, blue, curling smoke rose from her hand hanging over the edge of the tub. She appeared to be dozing. The room smelled strongly of pot. A smile spread across her face.

I backed as quickly out of the room as I could command my body to do it. Bill still chattered away about policies, etc., from the bed. I began to notice details in the room that I hadn't before. A single-edged razor blade balanced on a dusty mirror lying on the windowsill. Books, cigarettes, liquor bottles, and coffee cups covered every surface in the room.

I tripped on a crack vial as I ran for the door to the hall.

Collin Leech, Painter/Layout Artist/Set Designer
Age: 27
New York, New York

Too weird. . .I just woke up from a dream starring Bill Clinton. He was preparing for an acceptance speech or, perhaps, his inaugural speech. The dream constantly changed locations. . .Miami Beach. . .then somewhere else North. I knew it was North when I started seeing old red-brick walls. The dream had a feel of John Kennedy and Bill Clinton being one and the same at times. For some reason, I think that I was related to Bill Clinton—maybe a niece or a daughter. A lot of the dream has become foggy, except that he was waiting to give his speech. I and another, younger, female were to bring the speech to him where he was waiting. He looked more like a worn-out Ted Kennedy than the Bill Clinton we would all recognize.

There were CIA men everywhere, and they often came across as feeble. There was concern of an assassination attempt to be made. Finally, I was given the speech to deliver. Hours before, President Clinton had passed through the same secret passageway that I was about to enter. On a gravel rooftop there was a red-brick, cylinder-shaped entrance to the building below. I knew this was the same way Kennedy had passed for his speech—and it was here that Kennedy was killed.

First, the young female who was with me at all times passed through the secret passage for ordinary people, an entrance for the "help" only. This was a crawl space starting from what looked to be a sash window. Next, this passage led down a spiral staircase made of steel. There were CIA men at every step of the way. Finally, it was night. Since early A.M. President Clinton was waiting in this most secret part of the White House. When I made it down the passageway, there he was, in a gymnasium. And with the speech I handed him—off he went to present it.

Tess Pahl-Belitsky, House Cleaner/Art Student/Housewife
Age: 29
Miami, Florida

I was standing in a narrow white hallway of a corporate building, speaking with two men in the movie industry, when I noticed Bill Clinton walking down the hallway towards us, with two men close behind him. I was drawn towards him, and went to shake his hand, but he didn't see me. I could feel that had he seen me, he would have shook my hand like we were friends.

I then walked into the adjoining room, and was speaking with two girlfriends, when I felt a strong vibration which lasted ten seconds, then stopped abruptly. Bill had just began to walk into the room, but he stopped short and looked panicked. I said it was an earthquake and that he should have his men take him through the garage out to safety. One of my girlfriends said that it wasn't an earthquake, but just the garage, which causes vibrations. Bill stood there as if paralyzed—he didn't know who to believe.

Then came the big earthquake, strong and powerful, rocking the entire room. I screamed at Bill to leave, but he didn't move.

A round table with a sturdy center support came careening towards me, so I crawled under it for safety. It then went sliding towards Bill, so I told him to get under it with me, which he promptly did.

The table went sliding and spinning down the hallway, like a ride from Disneyland. We started to pass rooms depicting Bill's life. The first room showed him and Hillary in the White House. The next room showed Bill and Hillary when they were dating. The third room showed Hillary as a teenager in her parents' room, talking to her mom and dad.

It then struck me—his life is flashing before him. I asked him if he had died, and he looked me straight in the eye and nodded his head.

Judith Y. Malolepsy, Student
Age: 24
Los Angeles, California

I was going to my mother's house to house-sit for the weekend. After I got to her home, I sat down to watch some movies I had rented. I fell asleep and when I awoke I noticed I had been stabbed repeatedly.

When the police arrived, they suggested I go to the hospital, but I refused, because my friend was coming to pick me up to go to Ben and Jerry's to get ice cream.

The police let me go with her, and she didn't seem to care that I had multiple stab wounds.

She dropped me off at home, where I called my gram. I told her I had been stabbed and she said to me, "I warned you about him," and I asked, "Who?" She replied, "Bill Clinton, he's been going around stabbing people who have relatives in Arkansas."

I hung up the phone thinking that was very strange. Then I woke up.

Genevra Leo, Hairdresser
Age: 25
Orange, California

I, too, have a recurring dream about Bill Clinton. I am at work and it is exactly midnight. Suddenly, all these men in jogging suits come running through the doors with their guns drawn. Towards the back of this group are a few men carrying another man. When I see the guns, I am immediately scared to death. Then I notice that the jogger who is being carried is President Clinton! I can tell from the President's coloring that he is most probably suffering from a heart attack. As I jump up to help assist him, I am immediately struck on the back of the neck by a Secret Service agent who is yelling, "Do not touch the President!"

In my dream, I lay on the floor struggling, pinned down by security, knowing I am the only one who can help this great man and I am helpless to do so.

Jeff Pietsch, Nurse
Age: 40
Howell, Michigan

I was working in the laboratory—running a batch of blood tests on an instrument. The instrument would not operate, and people were very annoyed with me. I realized I had not identified the specimens, which were blood samples from Clinton's new cabinet members.

I did not know their names, and I had to consult a government textbook. I kept getting their names and jobs mixed up. Meanwhile, the instrument would not run, and my boss began proceedings to fire me.

Corliss Lundell, Medical Lab Technologist
Age: 46
Boise, Idaho

Presidential nominee Bill Clinton was visiting here in Portland, Oregon. I was downtown, waiting along with many other people outside a building in which Clinton was attending a meeting. Naturally, I was hoping to greet him when he emerged.

I was telling a woman standing next to me how much I admired him. Apparently, she was impressed with what I had to say, because she told me she was in Clinton's entourage and asked, "Why don't you join us when we leave here?" I was thrilled!

When Clinton exited the building, the crowd cheered and a long line of limousines began pulling up to the curb. He and his traveling companions hurriedly climbed inside, and the woman invited me to get in with her.

We hadn't gone far when I asked, "Where are we going?" (I thought we were going, perhaps, to another rally.) She replied, "To the airport, we'll be flying out right away."

Well, for me, leaving Portland was out of the question, and I said, excitedly, "Stop, please, and let me out!"

They stopped immediately. I got out and they quickly pulled away. When I looked around, I realized I was in the seediest area of downtown Portland. (In fact, I don't believe Portland has that seedy an area!) It was getting dark! The streets were bare and old buildings loomed tall and ominous.

I prayed to find a pay phone, or see a taxi or a policeman.

Then I noticed this old raggedy fellow walking haltingly up to me. I asked him if he could lead me to a phone. He didn't say a word but continued walking slowly away. I followed him.

He turned in to a building and went up a worn stairway and down a long, dimly lit hall. I followed. He opened a door, entered, and to my shock, shut the door in my face!

All this transpired, but he hadn't uttered one word or even acknowledged my presence. I had followed him on blind faith!

Panic-stricken, I turned and started to run from the building. Suddenly, a door opened and a young hoodlum with a long-bladed knife in his hand grabbed me. He started pulling me into the room!

G.M. (Female), Antiques Dealer
Age: 65
Portland, Oregon

Bill Clinton was friends with my neighbor Richie. Richie and Bill were both the same age, but they acted like little boys. I was friends with them, but my dad thought that they were bad influences on me, so I was not allowed to go out with them.

On the last day of school, it was very, very hot, and when I came home, my dad was at work. Bill was down at Richie's. He invited me down to sit on Richie's porch. When I got down to his house, there were lots of guys that I did not know. Then Bill offered me one of his different-sized cigarettes. So we sat in front of the house smoking differently sized cigarettes.

Suddenly, my dad came home. Both Bill and I became very scared that I would get in trouble for being with him. I ran home before my dad realized who I was with. He was still very mad at me because I had forgotten to do my chores. Next, my friend Tom pulled up in his Jeep Cherokee and wanted to go out to eat. We left really fast so that I would not have to listen to my dad yell at me anymore.

Jennifer Sauer, Student
Age: 15
Aurora, Colorado

I was entering a small apartment which in the dream was meant to represent Chelsea's rooms in the White House. I had been chosen as the only journalist allowed to interview Chelsea, but later I realized my role was really as her nanny. Hillary joins us in her daughter's rooms. At first, she is very cold and bitchy towards me, the help, but then warms up to me and becomes very friendly. The scene switches here to the White House pool.

As I come up to the surface, I notice that there are a lot of things happening around me, but I'm not sure what exactly is going on yet. Then I look to the left, at the far end of the pool, and I realize I'm seeing something I know I'm not supposed to see. Bill Clinton is in the pool with a couple of Secret Service agents, and a young blond woman. As I look over, I see him shove her under the water until she drowns. I begin to scream, but when I do, he looks up at me, and I realize I can't be left to be a witness to this murder. He comes over to me, and suddenly I am in a limousine with the President. He is sitting to the left, tied up and gagged, and I am sitting across from him, practically in his lap. I begin to make a deal with him, promising to release him if he agrees not to kill me. I then explain to him that I care very much for him and his family and that I have no intentions of telling anyone about the blonde.

L.G.H. (Female), Psychology Student
Age: 22
Virginia Beach, Virginia

I had this dream after watching President Clinton for two hours on TV in Arnold, Missouri, talking about the recent floods.

In the dream, my nine-year-old daughter and I were in Arnold, Missouri, and Clinton was wading through thick muddy water with hip boots on. My daughter, Molly, ran up to him and knocked him right over in the mud! She ran back to me and I said, "Molly Ann Malan, I can't believe you did that!" She was laughing hysterically and said, "I couldn't help it, Mom, it was too good to resist!" and continued laughing!

President Clinton got up after being completely submerged in mud. He was dripping thick mud head to toe; you couldn't see his face. The media went crazy and all you could hear was cameras clicking and my daughter laughing and me saying, "I can't believe you did that!"

Mary Malan, Unemployed
Age: 37
Greenville, Illinois

Out in the middle of a flat, barren stretch of land, there were these flights of steps not unlike the steps of a three-story home—there were no walls, no roof, no floor, only these three flights of steps, and I was the only one there temporarily. I had heard that President Clinton would be coming here for a speech, and I can remember being so excited about meeting him. I was standing on the top flight of steps, and I could see Air Force One approaching—there was no runway, not even a resemblance of an airport—only open land and dirt. I saw him get off the plane, naturally surrounded by Secret Service agents.

He started coming up the steps and I started descending the steps, and I kept thinking all the while that at some point we would meet on the steps and I would introduce myself. Somehow, we never crossed on the steps, and the next thing I knew, he was on the top flight and I was on the bottom. I remember standing down there looking up at him surrounded by agents waiting for him to speak. After what seemed an eternity, it became apparent there would be no speech, no nothing. Then he started ascending and again I figured we would meet at that certain point and I would get to talk to him, but instead we missed each other again, but he did look straight at me and smiled, and all the while he kept right on walking down the steps.

I remember feeling strange, like I was invisible or like I was on the outside looking in and no one even knew I was around. I watched him walk back toward the plane, but never really saw him enter the plane. I remember being so disappointed, so sad because I knew that this was one of those "once-in-a-lifetime opportunities" and it had just passed me by.

Reba McFarland, Manager of a Casualty Unit
for an Insurance Company
Age: 38
Greensboro, North Carolina

Performance Artists

Every Memorial Day weekend in Seattle they have a Folklife Festival that is free to the public and runs the entire weekend at Seattle Center, where the '62 World's Fair was held.

In this dream, I was going to Folklife just like every year, and when I got to the Center I picked up the tabloid, newsprint schedule. Events take place in various buildings all over the Center—some forty of them—and the schedule lists what's happening on the various schedules all three days. In this schedule, instead of listing musical entertainment, the schedule listed various members of the Clinton administration who would be giving talks on various topics all weekend long.

The Clinton administration had taken over the Folklife Festival. Only, no one seemed to mind. (Folklife draws your usual Birkenstock/vegetarian crowds.) So I attended this one forum that had Zoë Baird, Janet Reno, and the other woman nominated for attorney general (her name escapes me now!). They were talking about child care issues. Lloyd Bentsen gave a very interesting talk about the economy, and William Sessions was talking about CIA surveillance, while that Romeo-Juliet duo from the Bush-Clinton campaigns gave a dynamic workshop about how to make your relationship work against all odds.

The weekend was packed full of everything imaginable, with the highlight being Bill playing the sax in the Coliseum on Saturday night. The thing I most remember about this dream is how enthusiastic the crowd was. For a while, I was sitting by this large fountain that's in the middle of the Center, listening to wisps of conversations of people going by. Things like: "Oh my God, did you hear what Al Gore said about cleaning up the Sound?" and "That Leon Panetta, he really has a grasp of the situation. He feels the same as me."

There was this overwhelming feeling amongst "the people" that this man (Bill Clinton) and his entourage really, really care about the common people and are going to give us back control over our lives.

Karen Therese, Desktop Publisher
Age: 32
Seattle, Washington

I lived in a very nice neighborhood, and Bill lived across the street. We sat together on lawn chairs late one summer night, talking about politics. Then he asked if he could walk me home, and I said I thought I would be safe, but would he walk me home anyway so I could tell everyone about it. He held his arm out (like an usher at a wedding), and I put my arm through his, and he walked me home. I couldn't wait to tell my family.

Later, I did a beautiful dance routine with streamers of every color. I was hoping Bill would see me through the windows and be impressed.

Marty Lim, Dance Instructor
Age: 31
Lexington, Kentucky

I was in Washington, D.C., at a conference with Bill Clinton and his energetic young staff. In a meeting, I saw him naked and stretched out on a carpeted stairway or riser. He was talking. He lay on his stomach, then rolled over, managing to cover his penis as he turned, and he was still talking, making some point. Lots of people were listening.

Then I saw him sitting in a chair, clothed. There was a lot of stuff under his chair, including a Porky Pig comic book. I was given some papers and a metal box containing film or tapes that I was to return to Lani Guinier. One of Clinton's young aides put these in my hands and expected me to find Lani Guinier and give them to her, to mail them if necessary, and to send the Clinton staff the receipt.

Accompanied by a black man, I found Lani Guinier, and using a phony accent (almost like I was mocking her), I gave her the papers and the metal box and said, "Zee print ees too small." Then I was jostled along in a crowd. It was like a festival or a big party. I felt myself to be in my thirties, looking glamorous with long hair, and planning to meet my husband.

Finally, I saw myself naked at an altar in a large colorful party tent. It was night, after hours, after the festival. I had been meditating there for some time, it seems. The crowds were starting to return. I had to get myself together and get out of the tent. At a table, I found a used folder, red with a black logo. I took a marker and enlarged the logo and altered it slightly to make it look like a *C.* I was making a coupon to get myself admitted to some other event or situation.

J.H.P., Artist
Age: 57
Corpus Christi, Texas

Play One for Me, Bill

I had this dream while under general anesthesia for minor surgery in January 1993.

Clinton had gotten together with famous musicians he knows and made a CD of his saxophone music. It was for sale in all the stores. It was all donated time, so the entire cost of the tapes or CDs went directly to pay the national debt. The important thing was that he was President, so everybody wanted one. And to assure that all the money went towards the debt, there were no administrative costs, overhead, etc., etc. Not even the stores made a profit. Direct deposit.

M.E. (Female), Substitute Caller
for Rockford Public Schools
Age: 42
Rockford, Michigan

I was standing with a bunch of my friends on the corner of Forty-second Avenue South and Thirty-fourth Street in South Minneapolis, at a corner where there is a neighborhood bar, an auto repair shop, a small grocery store, and a standard brick apartment building. The neighborhood is basically residential, quiet. I suppose we were just waiting for the bus, standing there on the corner, as there's generally no reason to hang out there.

Standing on the corner by the apartment building, we saw Bill Clinton advancing toward us from over by the bar, with shades, black suit jacket, and saxophone. He played hot riffs on the saxophone as he walked toward us. We were totally groovin' to the music—I think people may have been clapping. The strange element to the moment was a menacing wild hog that was charging at us from time to time, which was of course quite distracting. We would back up while it charged and we didn't get hurt, but the music went on steadily.

David M. Jones, Professor of Composition and
African-American Literature/Musician
Age: 29
Minneapolis, Minnesota

In my dream, my husband, Jim, and I were going to a Neil Diamond concert. When we arrived, Neil Diamond was not there. Instead, there was an empty stage with a multicolored curtain. Playing over the loudspeakers were tapes of Bill Clinton singing Neil Diamond songs. My husband turned to me and said, "I think Bill Clinton is going to appear later and play his saxophone." I was horrified and replied, "Doesn't he have anything better to do?"

Veronica Morrison
Age: NA
Libertyville, Illinois

President Clinton was standing on a suspended stage playing his saxophone. I don't know the tune—but the sound was very soft and tranquil. I was fascinated by the iridescent tiny bubbles floating from the saxophone—they grew larger (size of a baseball) and then they burst and a cherublike angel came from each of them until there were hundreds of them floating around. And the President continued to play. It was as though light came out of darkness and shone on the President, and outside of the beam of light was darkness. President Clinton was dressed in a dark blue suit with white shirt and dark tie.

> **"Pat" Jean Whitehurst Pierce, Switchboard Operator**
> **Age: 58**
> **Charlotte, North Carolina**

The theater had a seating capacity of approximately four thousand, but there were only about two hundred people there, scattered in small groups all around the theater. On stage, Sting was giving a concert. (I personally loathe Sting and wouldn't be caught dead at one of his shows.)

But there I was, sitting by myself, and then I noticed that the man playing the saxophone in Sting's band was none other than Bill Clinton. I became very excited and started running around talking to everyone else in the theater. They were all friends of mine and people I went to high school with, but they were all ignoring me. I tried to get them to look at the stage and was telling them that Bill was up there playing, but nobody seemed to care. Then, just as Clinton ripped into a fantastic sax solo, Marv Albert came zooming out of the wings on a miniature flying saucer covered with lots of blinking lights. He flew around over the sparse crowd, posing like Elvis and shouting snippets of dialogue from the Coen Brothers' film *Barton Fink* into an old-style radio microphone, completely drowning out Bill's solo. I ran up the aisle to the stage, and just as I was jumping up onto it, the dream ended.

Nathaniel Haakinson, Student/Musician/Writer
Age: 21
Fort Collins, Colorado

In my dream, our Argentinian exchange student wants us to take her to Oaxaca. It is only one hour away, so we agree and hop in the car. On the way, we stop at McConnell Auditorium (on the campus of Central Washington University in Ellensburg, Washington) to see a symphony concert. The conductor makes an announcement that President-elect Bill Clinton will be taking over the first violin part. The song begins, and to me it sounds as if Clinton is doing a great job, but my father moans and groans and says it's a massacre.

So we get up to leave, and as we walk past the orchestra pit, I wave at Bill. His hair is all wet and he's dripping with sweat from the exertion, but he smiles and waves back at me. I spot Hillary and Chelsea in the front row of an otherwise empty theater, and I wave at them as well. Chelsea smiles beautifully and waves back, but Hillary takes no notice.

Jessaca Leinaweaver, College Student
Age: 17
Walla Walla, Washington

Romance

Shortly after the election, I had a dream that I had sex with Bill Clinton in the backseat of a car. In my dream, I knew he was married to Hillary, but I felt this overwhelming attraction for him and couldn't help myself. I asked him not to tell her about it. The strange thing about this dream is that in waking life, I don't find myself attracted to him. Incidentally, in my dream, he was *very, very* good.

Karen Therese, Desktop Publisher
Age: 32
Seattle, Washington

I was in my living room with Bill and Hillary and some other people, discussing the state of the nation. I was standing next to Bill, and he reached out to hold my hand. There seemed to be some sort of instant rapport between us. No one in the room noticed that we were holding hands. Then Bill asked to see my garden. We went out back, and suddenly my tiny California backyard turned into rolling hills and valleys. We wandered around and Bill told me how hard he was working and how discouraged he was at the criticism about his work. I told him how much I believed in him and that he should keep trying, that we were all depending on him. He said he needed someone to admit his weakness and fear to and that I was the most sympathetic listener he had met in a long time. He said Hillary was not always sympathetic.

I felt very close to Bill, and the dream was very erotic, but we didn't touch in the dream except to hold hands.

Katherine B. Lang, Software Technical Support Engineer
Age: 28
Mountain View, California

The first recollection I have is of riding with the President-elect, Bill Clinton, in the back of a black stretch limousine. We were sitting on the bench in the far back along with another woman. Bill sat in the middle. The woman was wearing a black sequined evening gown, and Bill was wearing a business suit. I'm not sure what I was wearing. Bill leaned over and whispered discreetly in my ear that he wanted me to be his mistress. As he said this his hand touched mine lightly. The first thing I thought was, "What if someone finds out?" It ran though my head that this would ruin not only his reputation but mine as well (not that I have one).

We (only Bill and I) were suddenly standing outside the limousine, which was parked on a dirt road edged with fields of tall brown grasses. The sky was overcast and it looked to be about dusk. Off to the right, there was a small farmhouse with a low barbed fence encasing another field of taller grasses and small trees and bushes. This house had a few rays of sun beaming down upon it. To the left, although I didn't see it, was the house where we were supposedly staying. I asked Bill about the woman who lived in the farmhouse and what would happen if she decided to tell someone about our affair. He went running into her field, jumping over the fence screaming that he would build her a higher fence and make her land a National Wildlife Refuge. He said that she was very into animal conservation, and if he did this for her, she wouldn't say anything.

M.G. (Female), Student/Secretary
Age: 25
Minneapolis, Minnesota

The dream took place in another city, but I don't know which. I was dressed provocatively and I was waiting for the President with a male Clinton staffer. The staffer indicated for me to open the door which led to a private bedroom where President Clinton was awaiting me. I don't remember any introductions or niceties. We immediately embraced and consummated the most erotic encounter.

After the fireworks, he quickly departed, leaving me feeling quite cheap. I also somehow knew in my dream that these rendezvous were arranged almost nightly with a different woman each time. I wondered how they kept it from the press, and especially from the First Lady.

Carmen Moody, Housewife and Mother of Three
Age: 36
Dallas, Texas

In my dream, I'm a young person, perhaps nineteen or twenty years old, and I have the same thoughts and feelings of the person I really am today. I'm in an open-windowed or windowless, unlit, cool office that is probably the sitting room or living room in an old, formal Southern plantation home. There is a wide overhang covering the front porch. The porch has a white wicker swinging seat, and ivy surrounds the open windows, porch roof, and painted posts. Ivy gently flows down the posts and, now that I think about it, flows down, and surrounds the screens that cover the windows of the home I'm in.

My job is clerical—filing, answering phones—not very significant. There doesn't appear to be any modern equipment being used—no faxes, PCs, etc. I am not alone in the office—there are other women working; we don't seem to really interact with each other.

I'm as excited as a young girl to get off work, because Bill is just outside the porch, must be standing in the gardens, visiting with many people as he waits for me. I am his "date"—I belong with Bill. He is dressed in a dark navy blue suit with a very white shirt and a cool colored tie. He looks very good and is very polished. He's also very relaxed and comfortable visiting while he waits for me. The sun shines on his face. He does not wear sunglasses. Others stand very close to him—he does most of the talking and laughing—he loves to laugh.

The surroundings outside are very green. The building and landscaping and feeling reminds me of a Southern plantation restaurant that I ate at in Kauai, Hawaii. Fans cooled the interior—big high fans. I felt the same in this plantation office room as I did eating in Hawaii—clean and cool and innocent.

Teresa St. Onge, Controller, U.S. Marines
Age: 41
Mukilteo, Washington

In my dreams, I am Bill Clinton's mistress. The entire White House staff knows, including Hillary. They all know and they don't care. In one dream, I was even invited and welcomed to state dinners. Nobody that worked at the White House cared what he did as long as he got his work done in the day. He would quite openly come home to ME after work every day.

J.E.E.
Age and Occupation: NA
Chicago, Illinois

About four months ago, I had a dream about President Clinton. He came over to me and asked me out. I said, "Why me? There's so many other women."

He said, "I guess I like your personality," and he put his arm around me. I woke up refreshed and happy!

Rita Townley, Teller
Age: 49
Milwaukie, Oregon

"1963," the huge plastic banner proclaimed. It flapped against the red and yellow tent, although there did not seem to be any wind. As I looked around I became aware that I was at a circus. Dry, dirty straw littered the ground, along with several crushed popcorn boxes and empty wax-coated Pepsi cups. Strange, though, there were only a few people around. They wandered list-lessly about, identical expressions of apathy on their faces. The atmosphere inside the tent, however, was one of excitement and joy. As soon as I pulled back the tent flap, a wave of cheers and shouts greeted me. Not a space on any of the bleachers was empty. People were pressed against each other so tightly that they had ceased to be individuals and were now just THE CROWD. They roared and stomped their feet as animals—elephants and tigers and monkeys—paraded through the center ring. As I stood just behind the bleachers closest to the tent flap, I spotted a dark-haired young man, about fifteen years old or so, hawking peanuts. I stared at him—where did I know him from? Then it hit me—he was Bill Clinton, the Democratic presidential candi-date! I ran over to him and exclaimed, "You're going to be President!"

He smiled calmly at me and said, "I know." Then he handed me a bag of peanuts. He seemed so sweet, so innocent. I realized suddenly that I was in love with him—something decidedly strange, because in my dream I was my twenty-four-year-old self and Clinton was a fifteen-year-old boy. However, the eight-year age difference didn't stop him from saying, "Will you marry me?"

Around us the crowd roared in approval—apparently they had been listening to our whole conversation. (How they all heard it is a mystery—dream acoustics, apparently.) Anyway, without wasting another moment. Clinton and I clasped hands and ran to the center of the ring. The elephants stampeded away in a panic.

The ringmaster, who looked eerily like Captain Stubing from *The Love Boat*, married us on the spot.

As we ran towards the tent flap, towards the pale sunshine out-side, popcorn fell on us like rice. Suddenly, from beneath the bleachers, Lucille Ball and Desi Arnaz tottered out in front of us. We nearly bowled them over! Rather than being young and attractive, as they would have been in 1963, they were old and withered. Lucille Ball gave us a long, measured look. When she spoke, her tone was sarcastic and bitter: "I know you will be as happy as Desi and I are."

After this little interlude with two of television's most famed personalities, the dream fades. I've thought again and again about how the dream ended, but I just can't remember. The last image I remember is turning to Clinton, perhaps to make a comment about how old Lucy was, and seeing his face not as the young, handsome boy's it had been, but as the haggard, defeated face of an old man harboring regrets. It was quite a startling and disconcerting end to what had otherwise been a playful and rather amusing dream.

Kim A. Gallagher, Community Development Assistant
Age: 24
Buena Park, California

It is a beautiful spring day. I am sitting in my backyard under a tree with Bill Clinton. He is telling me how very stressed he has become and how he cannot possibly please everyone. I murmur sympathy. He tells me that he has a splitting headache. I suggest that he lie down and relax. He sprawls out with his head in my lap. I ruffle his hair in a soothing manner. I am beginning to feel very affectionate towards him. He tells me that he is beginning to unwind. I say, "Forget about everything for now, just enjoy this beautiful day. Imagine that as I am stroking your hair, with each stroke your problems are sliding away." He thanks me for my kindness as I continue to stroke his hair (which is brown, not sprinkled with gray at all). He shuts his eyes. I feel very content.

174

I can hear birds chirping. As I realize that my feelings for Bill are deeper than I thought (I begin to think that I am falling in love!), Hillary appears, storming into the yard demanding to know what is going on. (She appears in the dream not as she looks on television or in print, but rather as almost a caricature or cartoon.) She is very jealous. Bill jumps up (almost hitting his head on a low-lying branch) and states that the situation is innocent. Hillary does not seem to be listening. She instructs me not to have further contact with the President and storms out of the yard, dragging Bill by the hand.

I watch as the pair walk up the long hill, atop which sits their home. I can see it from my backyard. There are no other houses aside from mine and the Clintons'. Their home is white and relatively modest. I can't remember any further details on what their house looked like, but suddenly my friend Richard appeared and said, "Well, they live right up the hill. Don't worry, you'll see him again." And I *am* worrying about seeing him again because I've realized that I am in love. Bill looks back and mouths, "See you later." I am ecstatic.

Stacy Wells, Legal Document Processor
Age: 25
Somerset, Massachusetts

Bill and I are in a pool. It reminds me of the YMCA—enclosed, tiled, steamy. We are holding on to the side with one hand and treading water, facing each other. A few men in dark suits are walking around. I assume they are Secret Service agents. I think to myself, "How did I get here?" Bill moves closer to me and says in a low voice, "Maybe you and I could get together later when

Hillary isn't around. I'll get you my room key." He nonchalantly moves his head toward the other side of the pool. I slowly look up, with a sense of dread. There is Hillary, sitting straight up in a chair, fully clothed in a power suit. She has her legs crossed, arms crossed, and she does not look happy. She is not looking our way, but I am frightened that she will notice us.

J.M. (Female), Homemaker
Age: 30
Wall, New Jersey

A couple of weeks before the election, I had a dream that changed my perception of Clinton dramatically. Just before I woke one morning, about seven A.M., I heard his voice in a dream. He said, clearly and in his distinctive Arkansas drawl, "I love you, J——," speaking my name and saying this with unquestionable sincerity. I could literally feel the love he had for me. It wasn't a sexualized love, but was affection and regard and respect, and conveyed his desire to do the best he could for me.

After I woke up, I could continue to feel the love, just as I can from some other intense emotional experiences in my life in which I've had absolute knowledge of someone's love for me.

I attended a rally for him four days before the general election. I went to the rally largely because my dream had puzzled me, and I hoped that seeing him in person again would help me understand it.

J.B. (Female), Psychophysiologist
Age: 42
Pittsburgh, Pennsylvania

In my first, Hillary and I were having a conversation about Bill and how I had feelings for him. We were down on the docks where she owned a business and she informed me that she was having an affair with a man named Steve. She was secretly saving money every week so that they could run away together after Bill's term was over, and said that I could have him to myself after that.

My second dream was that I was in a club and there was a party going on. I was having a good time chatting with my friends when Bill walked by and struck up a conversation with me. He asked me to have a drink with him and I said yes, so we strolled over to the bar and he bought me a drink. I turned to respond to a friend who called to me, and she asked me what in the world I was doing hitting on the President. Just then Hillary walked by and gave me a dirty look.

Nancy L. Whiting, Customer Service Representative
Age: 31
Fall River, Massachusetts

I am standing before the bathroom mirror, dressed in my bathrobe. Bill Clinton approaches me from behind. We follow one another's reflected, loving gazes in the glass. He slips his arms around me and nuzzles the right side of my neck. It's one of those tender, sensual, but nonsexual moments that husbands and wives share in the best of marriages. I feel loved, appreciated, and, above all, completely accepted for who and what I am.

D.S.M. (Female), Writer
Age: 37
Salt Lake City, Utah

Bill was my BOYFRIEND! I remember holding hands, smiling at him, him smiling back, and kissing him (short kisses).

The dream was in color and, when I awoke, seemed very real. I could still feel him. He was very sweet and always smiling. I cannot remember where we were, but we were alone.

Yvonne Myers, Housewife/College Student
Age: 33
Brighton, Michigan

Bill Clinton and I were having an affair. We were at a party and I didn't know anybody there. I went up behind a man that I thought I knew and gave him a hug from behind and asked, "How are you doing?"

He turned around and it was someone I didn't know. Bill saw it happen and came over to me and said, "Let's go get something to eat." We went to a restaurant and it was packed; there was only one table left and it was a corner booth. As we were walking to the table, I noticed that sitting at a table next to ours was an old high school classmate of mine. I thought, "Oh, shit."

I felt kind of funny introducing him and saying, "This is Bill Clinton." We talked for a while, then Bill got called off to an emergency meeting. My high school classmate said, "Boy, have I got gossip to tell Lexington."

And I said, "There's nothing to tell yet!"

C.D. (Female), Assistant Buyer
Age: 33
Charlotte, North Carolina

I was having an affair with Bill Clinton. We were attending a meeting in a conference room where I work. Included in the meeting were Hillary and some of Bill's top aides. Hillary left the meeting momentarily, and I took the opportunity to search through her purse while she was gone (I have no idea what I was searching for). Shortly after she came back, the meeting broke up, and everyone was preparing for their trip back to Washington—everyone but me, that is.

Consequently, I was becoming extremely worried about being left behind when one of Bill's aides came to me and said, "Bill told me to tell you to catch the next plane out of here to Washington." I was, no doubt, relieved, and then woke up.

Jacquelyn S. Beck, Secretary
Age: 45
Houston, Texas

science Fiction

I am sitting in the back of a limo with Hillary, Bill, and my wife, Annette. We're zooming along and Bill says he needs a vacation. I suggest he come up to Pine Mountain, our country house, after he is elected. Bill asks, "Do they have a helicopter pad?" I answer, "Yes, they do." Annette and I are at the helipad when Bill's helicopter, which looks like *Star Trek's Enterprise*, lands. Bill gets out and puts his arm around me and we go into the Town Meeting. Everyone is blown away that I am with the President like this. Then Bill says to me, "It's too crowded. Why don't we go back to your place." Which we do.

Alan Sacks, Producer
Age: 50
Hollywood, California

Here in Austin, Texas, there is a coffeehouse/sidewalk cafe called Captain Quackenbush's. A lot of students and intellectuals hang out there, and have discussions, poetry readings, etc.

In my dream, Bill Clinton and George Bush were having a debate at Captain Quackenbush's. I don't remember what exactly was said in the debate, but I knew in the dream that it was very important, that the outcome of it would decide the election.

This was kind of crazy because there were no reporters or news crews present, nor was there a big crowd. Just the two candidates, me, and maybe six or seven other people who didn't even seem to be paying attention.

After the debate, Bush got into a limousine and was driven away without talking to anyone. Clinton, on the other hand, came to my table and asked if he could buy me an espresso. We sat there together drinking our coffee, and he kept asking me what I thought of the debate, particularly his prochoice stand on abortion.

I was thinking, "This is *unreal.* I can't believe he's actually talking to me. I'm going to be famous. The media will probably say that we're having an affair or something."

One thing that Bill kept repeating was, "Do you think I'm coming off honest? Do you think I sound sincere?"

He kept asking me that over and over, and I kept reassuring him that he did, but he didn't seem to believe it.

Bill had a bag of Hershey's chocolate chips, and we were dropping them a few at a time into our coffee, where they melted into sludge. It made the coffee taste really good.

Suddenly, the lady at the table next to us screamed and fell out of her chair, clutching her stomach.

At first, I thought she was having a baby or something. She kept screaming and all of a sudden the sky got really dark and overcast.

"I think we should get her to the hospital," I told Bill.

But he just smiled and kept on talking as if he hadn't noticed the woman, who was writhing around on the floor a few feet away from our table.

Suddenly, the woman's stomach burst open, and an alien came out (like in the movie *Aliens*).

It skittered across the floor of the cafe and disappeared beneath a table. Nobody in the room seemed concerned. They were all very nonchalant about it. The lady on the floor got up, covered with blood and with a big gaping wound in her abdomen, sat back down at her table, and continued her conversation.

I asked Bill, "What are you going to do about *that* if you get elected? We certainly can't have things like that going on in America."

Bill kind of changed the subject and started talking about taxes and the defense budget and other unrelated issues.

Suddenly the alien, which was about the size of a house cat, jumped up onto our table. I screamed, and Bill just laughed.

Then the alien leapt up and attached itself to Bill's face. He just calmly kept talking, although his voice was kind of muffled. I was petrified, but I had this idea in my head that I had to act normal, that everything would be okay as long as I didn't let on that I was scared.

Finally, Bill said that he had to go. He got up and pushed in his chair and started walking away.

"Bill!" I called.

"Yes?" He turned around.

"Bill, you've got an alien stuck to your face!"

Everyone in the cafe laughed, but they were laughing at me, not at him, as if I was ignorant and crass to have mentioned such a thing. "It's okay," Bill said calmly, "it's been spayed."

Then he just waved and walked out the door.

H. W., Homemaker/Student
Age: 20
Austin, Texas

I went over to my boyfriend's house, and he and his sister were sitting on the couch looking very astonished. I asked what was wrong and they told me the President had AIDS. I ran home to tell my mother this, and she was in the kitchen opening mail. She opened an envelope which contained a big news-flyer stating that Mr. Clinton had AIDS. We then sat down to watch the news. Of course, this was the leading story. The reporters said that the President had contracted AIDS in a way researchers had never heard of before. He was handling some papers with a newly developed type of ink that causes AIDS. Then they announced that the flyers sent out by the President were printed with that ink.

Sara Nacy, Student
Age: 18
Milford, Michigan

A crowd of neighbors were gathered on the shore of Lake Minnetonka. They kept glancing at the afternoon sky, looking for space shuttle debris which was expected to fall to earth nearby. I looked up in time to see a flaming piece of the hull come shooting out of the sky and hit the water. I waded in for a closer look. The water felt warm, heated by the debris. When the debris had cooled down, a few people dragged it out of the water and hauled it away on a tractor which they had hidden. I didn't think they were authorized to take it, so I noted what they looked like and that two names were painted on the tractor: "Lou & Kathy."

I then proceeded to an elementary school, where Bill and Hillary Clinton were appearing in the school gym. Hillary was speaking, but she seemed to be having trouble saying what she had to say in front of Bill. She said to him, "Oh, baby, just get out of here." He was a good sport and got down off the stage and left the gym. Hillary's mood immediately lightened. It had all been a ruse to get him out of the room so she could coordinate our participation in a surprise for him.

L.M. (Female), Employee Benefits Specialist
Age: 30
Roseville, Minnesota

I have at least one dream per week where Bill Clinton is involved (that I remember).

Usually, the President is a substitute for other people in my life, and the dreams aren't that spectacular. I remember last week's dream because it left an "evil" feeling after I awoke.

In my dream, I stood in a crowd in Golden Gate Park (San Francisco), which included Barbara Bush, Truman Capote, and William F. Buckley. Our attention was focused on a jogging path when Bill Clinton jogged by. His legs were very white and chunky. I asked Barbara if this meant it was okay now to be overweight, and she hissed at me.

I turned back to look at the President, and suddenly his jogging shorts fell down around his ankles. He was now jogging and "mooning" the crowd of observers. Someone yelled, "The Emperor has no clothes!" I somehow saw the wisdom in this, but was very agitated, since I'd voted for Clinton, and like him. Barbara Bush said, "Look! He's a robot." Just then, Clinton came apart. . .his arms fell off, his chest opened up, and there were springs and wires sticking out of his body. Truman Capote then turned into Nancy Reagan, with glowing red eyes. She screamed, "It's all YOUR fault, you voted for him!" I tried to get away, but William Buckley and my husband pulled my hair, smothering me in the crowd. I awoke with my face embedded in my pillow, and lay awake for a few hours after that.

Deborah L. Peeples, Retail Clerk
Age: 41
Redwood City, California

I dreamt I was going to pat Bill Clinton on the head. As I reached out and touched his hair, it turned into cool green spongy moss.

Peggy Shaw, Video Producer/Artist
Age: 35
Tolono, Illinois

I had the following dream several days after attending a gathering on the beach in Honolulu, where President Clinton spoke to an estimated 21,000 people.

President Clinton was walking on the beach where he had spoken. There were no crowds, and the beach area was deserted. Behind the President followed a small group of native Hawaiian people, dressed in traditional garments. When they got to the ocean, which was very choppy, the President lifted his arm and the waters parted. He motioned for the people to follow, but they held back. He moved forward into the parted water and looked back, smiling, to assure the others that they would be safe.

S.F.L. (Female), Legislative Aide in City Government
Age: 58
Honolulu, Hawaii

I'm at a gathering or party with strange people. One man warns me about a spaceship; he tells me that I belong on the spaceship and they are going to come and get me.

I'm with another man who's helping me move, very gentle. We're trying to move and this gray gunmetal spaceship swoops in and hovers in front of the big window warning me that they're on their way.

"They're coming to get you now!" the first man said.

At first, I didn't believe him, when I met him at the party, but now that he's come in a spaceship, I believe it. I am panicky and try to find my clothes and get dressed before they come. (In another part, I think I am naked but it turns out that I do have clothes on.)

Immediately this second spaceship, a hippie kind of ship made of all kinds of odds and ends, not at all slick, sweeps over and hovers in front of the window. And this very powerful, big woman looking at me says in a derogatory way, "She's not so much!"

The people are people I have seen before. Once I get on the ship, it's friendly and so I have a feeling of belonging there. There's no more sense of threat. There is all kinds of food laying around on tables inside the spaceship. Very raggle-taggle place made of odds and ends.

I ask them where they're from and they say "the planet X Leon" (or something like that) in a matter-of-fact way, like there's nothing surprising about the way they live.

In the spaceship, a group of young men are talking about making music and how they need bells and flutes and other instruments. I ask if they have a synthesizer. They say no. I tell them about my two keyboards and think about sharing them.

I'm in the spaceship. I've just dropped a piece of chocolate cake. I'm wiping the floor but I discover that I can hover above it and with my feet send out this energy that cleans it up. The powerful woman comes in and asks me if there is anything I have to do today.

I say, "I don't have to do anything, but I have to do something and I'm not sure what it is and that's the most difficult." We both laugh.

The powerful woman looks human but has strange, slanted, somewhat alien eyes and hippie/bohemian "grunge" clothes.

I leave to teach and find myself levitating down steep stairs. I pretend that I am walking so as not to attract attention, but I am sweeping down over them and hovering. I have this power to send energy from my feet and ride on it. Like an antigravity device. Then I'm in a car in a university area. But men with baseball bats line the streets, and they are threatening cars that pass through. But they suspend violence and I pass through and go to my classroom. I've noticed that my class roll sheet has information about whether the students voted for Clinton. I decide not to read it, because I don't want to be prejudiced toward people who didn't vote for him. At the table, we're talking about the new administration and Clinton, except that I say "Kennedy." He appears before us and he has this shining sign or epaulet on his left arm, and I know that it represents the passing on of some sacred sign or badge.

I'm at a crowded restaurant with Hillary and Bill. We are laughing and talking like intimate old friends. There is a feeling of kinship and great well-being and humor—that the world is really all right.

Sara Deutsch, M.S., CHT, Psychotherapist
Age: 50
Fairfax, California

snacks

I lived across the alley from President Clinton. I don't know whether he had just moved in or not, but I had not known him before. My house was the house where I lived (in Moline, Illinois) for thirty years, until 1985. The house that Clinton had was in back across the alley to the right. We (I don't know who I was with, but it seemed to be a man) went to visit.

We walked into his house, entering through a screened-in porch. It was a house I was not familiar with. It was very light. There was a swimming pool. He had a wife and children or child. There seemed to be a dog also. They were really friendly and gave us a snack of some sort, which they served on the coffee table, and a tour of the house. Clinton was in shirtsleeves and didn't act like a President. He was Mr. Average and said he was happy we came to visit.

Marjory A. Buckingham, Professional Event Planner
Age: 62
Findlay, Ohio

Bill Clinton came into the room where I was having breakfast—kind of a cafeteria. He wore a suit and tie; people applauded. Fragments (of the dream): I'm looking at an old, thick, dark red book, *The Cambridge History of Europe: 1940*, and I am told that it's his favorite book; I talk to him about it, he likes it because 1940 was right at the edge of World War II. Meaning, as I recall, that it was a "threshold" year, not quite in and not quite out, where decisions have a particularly crucial impact on the course of history.

I tell him the trouble with wars is both sides always claim to be fighting for justice, and usually neither really is. More talk about various things, often referring to books which I sometimes also have read. His aides are there, too, at another table close by. He makes up a joking ditty to them: "I am the very model of a modern major-general," then two lines that scan and rhyme (don't I wish I could remember them exactly!) about if you don't come to my ball, I'll soak your head in the fountain.

M—— G—— (a friend of mine with a notoriously sensitive ego) is eating at a table across from me. George Stephanopoulos jokes that M—— will be good for bringing kindness and gentleness to the administration; M—— does not respond. A remark from aides about how many people from Cupertino and Black Mountain (California) are involved with the administration.

I have to say that this sure beats the dreams I used to have about the last two administrations. Most of those had to do with nuclear war!

Steven C. Rasmussen, Computer Musicology
Age: 34
Cupertino, California

I dreamed Bill made me a ham sandwich from a beautiful sugar-cured whole ham. But it was on white bread like Wonder bread (yuck). Nice spicy mustard, real vine-ripened tomato, and green lettuce. He handed it to me on a china plate and said, "That'll be one hundred sixteen dollars, please."

Barbara Gillies, Saxophonist for Hidden Colors
Age: 36
Chicago, Illinois

The first thing I remember was standing on a yacht, in the midst of a party. I could hear music playing in the background over the conversation and laughter at the black-tie event. As I walked toward where I could hear the music coming from, someone from behind me said, "Excuse me, would you care to dance?"

When I turned around, in that slow dreamlike sense, I realized it was Bill Clinton who had asked me the question. So I nodded my head yes, then he took my arm and led me to the dance floor. Seeing as how I'm not the most politically correct person, conversation was light. I'm not sure of the music we were dancing to, some kind of waltz, or where Hillary was, for that matter, all I could think was, "Oh my God, I can't wait to tell my mother that I danced with the President of the United States."

When the song ended, Bill asked me if I was hungry. I said yes, and he said he knew of a great place to eat. So I followed him out into the hallway, which had an elevator that took us up to the roof of a skyscraper, that was at one time the yacht that we were dancing on.

On the roof already was a red-checkered blanket laid out with what looked like calamari, scampi and mushrooms, and bread (appetizers from the Italian restaurant that I used to work at in real life). As we enjoyed the food, I wondered, how exactly was I invited to a party with the President, and why am I eating calamari with him, watching the sun set beyond the city skyline?

I must have fallen asleep, because the next thing I remember was waking up, still on the roof, but Bill was gone, and the unfinished calamari, to my chagrin, was cold. So I stood up, straightened my dress, headed for the elevator, and that was the end of my dream.

After having this particular dream, I am so inspired to read the newspaper because I wouldn't want to get caught in the above situation and not know what's going on in the world.

Leigh Ronnow, Temporary Receptionist
Age: 22
Denver, Colorado

I watched Bill Clinton deliver his Democratic Convention address *with a bunch of women friends in Baltimore, where we were attending a conference.*

That night I dreamed that Bill took all of us bowling. None of us bowl, mind you, but in my dream Bill was there to make it all right. He was courteous—holding the door, cheering every time we knocked over a pin, making sure our shoes fit, and buying us greasy hamburgers and french fries—and we had a wonderful time with him.

He was a rare man, a man who knew how to make a woman entirely at ease and as though we were known to him and liked.

However, I knew he really was interested in me, and the attention and courtesy he showered on my friends was only because he could do nothing else. In the back of his mind, I was the only one for him. (Maybe as a Democrat from UTAH, I am used to being unique.)

It was a thoroughly pleasant dream that ended with a hot tub experience.

Rebecca Heal, Fund-raiser
Age: NA
Salt Lake City, Utah

My older brother and I were standing in a meeting room with Bill Clinton somewhere in the White House with three other very important-looking men who I suspected were cabinet members or advisers to the President. My brother, John, was in conversation with President Clinton, and was actually advising him on how some of the bottom-line figures in one of his budgets was derived. I remember standing there, thinking, "Well, John is an accountant and has somehow worked himself into finalizing a business project budget with President Clinton, but what in the heck am *I* doing here?" I'm a family-practice physician and have been keeping up with Hillary Clinton's proposals regarding national health care. I wondered if I was going to have a chance to have some input into physician concerns about national health reform, but was mesmerized in watching the one-on-one conversation take place between my brother and President Clinton.

Suddenly, Bill Clinton dropped a Snickers bar he had been holding (which I hadn't noticed until it left his hand). In an instantaneous reflex, my brother reached out and caught the

Snickers bar before it hit the ground. Bill looked at John in amazement and said, "Good catch, John. That was really a damn good catch." John handed the candy bar back to him, undaunted.

I stood there, frozen and jealous, thinking, "That's just about the most awesome move John could have ever made for his career." I never got a chance to talk to anyone in the dream, but when I woke up, I had an overwhelming desire to call my brother and tell him how impressed I was.

Dave Westrup, M.D., Family Practice
Age: 38
Longview, Washington

I had a very vivid dream about President Clinton. We were in a huge, old-fashioned (almost medieval) kitchen. It was dark, as if it were underground. There was a huge fireplace with a fire roaring and a lot of activity. President Clinton was the lord of this manor, and, in the dream, I was very upset with him because I wanted his favor but he told me, and I understood intuitively, that I first had to do as he told me to.

My task was to clean these huge cast-iron pots which were coated with bacon fat. I was really unhappy with this (being a vegetarian in real life), but I understood that it was necessary to do this—that we had some kind of karma to work out, so to speak, and I had to do my dirty work.

Eva Baker, Bookkeeper
Age: 42
Columbus, Ohio

Squabbles, Fights, and Arguments

I am trying to sleep, but I have to wake up because something is wrong. The bed is huge and I am way on one edge of it, and Hillary is sitting at the bottom edge with her head in her hands. There is a small black-and-white TV in the corner of the room with a bad late-night movie on. Hillary is distressed and it's my job to help her, but nothing works. I offer to rub her back and she lets me, but it doesn't do any good. Bill is out in the hall in a ratty blue bathrobe, and every so often he paces past the door grumbling under his breath.

I try to get him to come in and talk, but he won't. He's being very petty. Finally, he goes into the other room and plays video games for the rest of the night. Hillary just sits there not knowing what to do, and I sit with her. I feel like a failure. I am afraid they will get divorced and it makes me sad, because I thought they could have done some really good things for all of us if they could only have learned how to get along. The sun starts to come up with Bill still in the other room. Hillary and I finally pass out from exhaustion.

D.B.J. (Female), Computer Programmer
Age: 23
Minneapolis, Minnesota

Bill Clinton and a black man were walking on the sidewalk of Albert Pike Avenue, a street in Fort Smith, Arkansas, where I grew up. The two of them got into an argument about race relations. I don't remember the details of the argument, but it got quite heated. I was within earshot of the argument. Race relations are something I feel strongly about, so the argument upset me. It upset me so much that I immediately went to Hot Rod's high school history class to speak to his students about race relations.

Hot Rod was the nickname of a childhood friend of mine who happened to be black. We both graduated from Fort Smith Northside High School, but he went on to the University of Central Arkansas, where he obtained a degree in history. He ended up teaching at Fort Smith Northside.

Jeremy Partin, Actuary
Age: 26
Little Rock, Arkansas

On July 4th, 1992, I dreamed that some representatives from Ethiopia were giving me three small silver medallions for my efforts in trying to encourage Bill Clinton to acknowledge or attend the formal burial of the remains of Ras Tafari, Haile Selassie I. Then Bill and I were in some small corner parking lot of some run-down little Arkansas town. His suit coat was unbuttoned and we were having a disagreement. He had other things to do, and he didn't want to think about anything else.

Lex Nuss, Corporate Security
Age: 40
Little Rock, Arkansas

I was at home walking through the kitchen when there, sitting on the kitchen table, was one those old countertop hockey games. This was like the very one we had at work in the late seventies when we held frantic tournaments during break and lunch periods.

At the time, I was really hot and won several of the tournaments, but since then I hadn't played in years. Now here was one of those games, well used, and with the same flat tin guys missing paint where the sticks always hit the puck.

So now, who comes walking in but Bill Clinton! Instead of being there for any particular reason or explaining his presence, he just comes walking through like he's on his way somewhere else. Then he spots the hockey game, turns smiling, and begins to reminisce in his soft friendly voice. "Boy, we used to have one of these, and I played it all the time. I got pretty good, too." So now we both start playing. We're wildly grabbing and twisting rods, sending the skinny tin men and the puck all over the rink. Bill was getting frustrated and raised his voice to be heard over the clatter. "I can't find my guys! Every time I find the right rod, the puck is across the board somewhere."

The dream ends up with the game, a total rout. *I woke up feeling really good and remembering my dream in vivid detail (which almost never happens). I told my wife, "You won't believe the dream I had. . .I just whipped Bill Clinton's butt playing tabletop hockey!"*

Tom Frey, Aircraft Windshield Mfg. Plant Executive
Age: 40
Murrysville, Pennsylvania

I was in a parklike setting, and although I am sixty-five years old, I appeared in my dream to be thirty years younger. Bill

Clinton was dressed casually, in a short-sleeved shirt and khaki tan pants.

I was walking rapidly away from him as he followed me, keeping pace. I was yelling at him, "You damn fool! You could have been the best President this country has ever had. You goofed! You promised to do good, now you are doing the opposite!"

He replied clearly, "Oh, give me a chance!"

Lt. Col. Felix E. Turtur, USAF, Retired
Age: 65
Manahawkin, New Jersey

I rarely dream of well-known personalities. I dreamed of David Niven about twenty years ago and Bill Curtis ten years ago!

I was working in an office setting (strange because I am a nurse). It was very dark—I was standing in a hallway and a group of people came down the hall. I was asked to give President Clinton a tour of the building. At first, I politely declined, but was pressured and finally said, "No!" emphatically. There was a short conversation which I don't remember. He handed me an autographed picture of himself which I also declined and walked away.

Cathy Junor, Nurse
Age: 44
Villa Park, Illinois

My husband and I were included in a close circle of friends of Bill and Hillary. They decided to have an intimate dinner party of their group of friends. In the dream, we must have lived in D.C., because we all drove over in our cars, and we all parked in the White House drive and on the lawn as well.

About three quarters of the way through the dinner (at a huge banquet table), Bill and Hillary got into a huge argument. They were screaming (and cussing) at each other across the table and in front of everyone (I don't know what the argument was about). All the guests decided to leave right then. Well, just about the time everyone (twenty to thirty people) got outside on the lawn, a big thunderstorm hit. People were running for their cars in all directions. It began lightning and three people were struck. My husband and I gave CPR to the victims, with help from four or five others. There was a bush burning nearby.

Lots of ambulances and big red fire trucks came, and they took over resuscitation (Bill had called them). As we drove away, I saw the White House with fire trucks and ambulances.

Beverly Hurst, Department Store Manager
Age: 35
Harvey, Louisiana

The setting was a large comfortable room in the White House with many sofas and soft chairs. Hillary Clinton was seated on a small sofa against one wall. It was five or six P.M. and she had been working hard all day. Now she was angry with Bill about something and was sulking. Bill said he was going to have a drink and headed for a table with a decanter. I thought, "Oh, my God! Is he really going to do that?! What if there's a crisis to attend to, and he's been drinking?!" But he didn't make a drink. Instead, he and Hillary sat down on a couch toward the middle of the room and talked things over amicably. I was glad that the few other people in the room saw this mature behavior.

Vicki Bruns Briggs, Artist/Library Clerk
Age: 49
Champaign, Illinois

Teeth

I was in an organic chemistry lab, and Bill was my teacher. We were doing a procedure having to do with tooth enamel. Bill was going over the main points of the experiment. He handed out a procedural guideline to each of us, then pulled out a specimen tray with two large molars in it.

I began to complain that I was not interested in tooth enamel, and that I wanted to study some reactions involving wood fiber and cellulose degradation. Bill just looked at me with a condescending glance and continued with his discussion about the chemical structure of tooth enamel and how we would be using tooth enamel as a representative compound to study the effects of some double-replacement reactions involving free radicals.

I quit complaining and started getting into the discussion.

Then, as I began to do the experiment, I remembered that Bill was now the President-elect of the United States. A warm, reassuring feeling overcame me as I realized that my chemistry teacher was the President, and I decided that I must be attending a good school if one of my professors could be elected President!

When the experiment was over, we had all transformed our molar specimens into four big front teeth, which we each inserted into our mouths. Then when I looked around the room, I saw that we all had big smiles just like President Bill, and he was smiling too.

Kevin Wahl, Student
Age: NA
Minneapolis, Minnesota

I was bragging to all my friends that I knew the President. "Oh, come on," they'd say, "you're full of it." "No, really," I insisted, doubting for a moment that I actually did know him. Then it came to me: He was my dentist, that's what it was. After I stated this fact, there was no longer any doubt about my veracity. "Everybody" was aware that President Clinton, in his attempt to prove that he is "one of the people," had made a point by continuing to practice dentistry even after occupying the White House. So, in addition to attending to all the duties of the presidency, he also operated his dental practice. Of course, he only saw the patients that he had seen before running for President. I, being lucky enough to have been one of them, continued to regularly see President Clinton for dental checkups. In fact, I had an appointment coming up.

I arrive at the dentist's office too antsy to sit in the waiting room. I am surprised that the receptionist does not try to stop me when I walk past her towards Bill. Dressed in his white coat, he is scurrying around busily, looking at X rays and checking on patients. He is reading an X ray when he spots me out of the corner of his eye, seems extremely happy to see me, and drops everything to escort me to an examining room. Bill is in no hurry to ask me to sit in the dentist's chair. I notice that he is standing just a bit too close to me, so I take a couple of steps backward, bumping into a wall, and smile awkwardly.

"So how's it going?" he says.

"My teeth are fine," I answer, trying to keep the conversation businesslike. Ignoring my teeth, he pastes on an ear-to-ear smile, and says something like, "Teeth shmeeth." He reaches his arms out towards me and bends to place his lips near mine. Although I am very tempted to respond, I duck under his arms and squirm away. He quickly gets the message and does not persist in his advances. He doesn't say a word, but his rejected expression asks, "Why?"

"I don't want to be like Gennifer Flowers! They'll paste my face all over the newspapers and call me a bimbo!" I say out loud. Bill gestures towards the dentist's chair, and I agree to sit down. He places the nitrous oxide mask over my face and, as the effects begin to take hold and he is drilling away at my teeth, I think about how angry Hillary would be if she found out, and how terrible I would feel hurting her like that.

When I get home later, all I can think about is that I missed the opportunity to have an affair with the President. I'm so angry I could kick myself. I could have been like Marilyn Monroe, singing for his birthday.

Alyce Wittenstein, Filmmaker
Age: 30
Forest Hills, New York

Hillary Clinton had just undergone mouth surgery, and she had bloodstains all over her sequined pajamas. I'm serious!

Peter Jennings was there, too, doing something fake.

Anyway, Bill was extremely agitated by all of the commotion, and was frantically looking for the Bible he was sworn in with. I guess he wanted to look up some advice. I had hidden it.

The reason I know I had this dream is this: My computer wakes me up three times a night with a soft female voice politely asking, "What are you dreaming, Mike?" The microphone over my bed records my groggy, sleepy-headed response. It works quite well.

Michael Price, Student
Age: 19
Minneapolis, Minnesota

The Love that Surpasseth Understanding

My dream of Bill took place in a large elegant hotel ballroom, or a grand room in the White House where a social gathering might take place. There were maybe fifty to one hundred people there, all relaxed, talking, enjoying and laughing. The women were very dressed up, and the men wore suits. Everyone knew each other, and there was no pretense or phoniness among us. There was soft music in the background, soft jazz: piano, sax, bass, soft brushes on the drums. The hall had two levels, there were twenty steps or so up to the second level, and I could see the crystal champagne glasses sparkle, and all the people above enjoying and laughing.

I was standing with Bill on the lower level. We were talking, but not with words. We were communicating through our thoughts only. It was not a "physical thing," but more a spiritual connection, as if we had known each other forever. He leaned in to hold me in his arms, and we hugged for a long, long time. Time seemed to stop, and everyone around us went into slow motion. We stayed like this for a very long time. It was the warmest and most complete and whole feeling I've ever experienced, even in real life. You could compare it to the end of your relationship with your first true love, knowing you had to say goodbye, but knowing you would never feel this deeply again. It was a very spiritual moment.

Finally, I pulled away from him slightly, looked up at him, and said (with thoughts, not words), "Hillary is on the landing," which she was! I was surprised. She looked beautiful as she stood laughing with some friends. She had her back to us, but we could see the profile of her face.

He looked back to me and said with thoughts, "It's okay because she doesn't really care." I looked at her again, and saw that she was totally self-absorbed, but not in a negative way. We resumed our hug for a very long time, and nobody around us really cared. It seemed to last for my whole night's sleep, and it seemed that night as if I was sleeping for a whole week! The feeling was so incredible that even to this day I can recall that lovely time, that peace, that serenity, that joy and feeling of completion and wholeness.

The dream ended that way, and I guess I could compare it to the way I feel during prayer and meditation, except that, then, there is nobody else involved, it's just me and God. I believe that Bill Clinton is a very old soul, and has been here many times before, and that I, in another life, knew him well.

Donna Bennett, Dancer/Choreographer
Age: 32
South Windsor, Connecticut

P resident Clinton and I were talking about having an affair. We were attracted to one another, and a sexual and emotional energy danced between us. We felt a deep bond, so that words were not necessary. In fact, most of our conversation was done telepathically. We talked about whether or not an affair was a practical idea, and, finally, we both decided that it was not in our best interest, especially since he was the newly elected President. We hugged, and I felt as if we had known each other for a very long time. He was kind, and even in my dream he was soft-spoken.

It is important to say that it was not the situation of a starstruck, ordinary person gushing over the President-to-be. The situation held two adults, speaking openly and honestly.

Ever since that dream, my compassion for his position as President has grown dramatically.

Tambra Nelson, Writer/Mother
Age: 33
Longmont, Colorado

weddings

I was at a friend's wedding outdoors in the green grassy yard of a farmhouse when it began to rain. All of a sudden, we were in a big church. The groom sat at a long wooden table with male friends on both sides of him. It looked like the Last Supper. President Bill was sitting two seats to the left of the groom.

I came walking in and I lay down on the floor under a podium directly across from the groom. The groom was shy of all the attention he was getting, so when I walked in, he turned the attention to me. He commented on how nice my slippers were and asked if they were made out of ostrich fur and asked me to tell how I had made them, since he knew that I was a tailor.

I started telling the story of how I had made my ostrich fur slippers, and it was evidently a very funny story, because everyone was still laughing and laughing, and that's when President Bill looked at me and his eyes bugged out and his hair stood straight up and he practically exploded with joy and laughter. He turned to the groom and they started talking about the weather or something, and I slipped into the back room of the church.

Now there was a church lady in the back room who was gripping a small table. Her knuckles were white and she looked very tense. I tried to make some light small talk when she interrupted me and said, "This is a very holy place!" We were both looking out at the table where the groom was still talking to Bill. I said, "That is a holy place out there, but in here it is evil."

She seemed shocked at my apparent disrespect for the church. So I said that I could prove it to her. There was a thick rope hanging into the middle of the room which I figured was from the belfry. So I said, "Watch this." I said, "HELL'S BELLS," and the rope started swinging. I said, "HELL'S BELLS...HELL'S BELLS...HELL'S BELLS..." and the rope started swinging violently at the church lady and she had to run out of the way. I kept saying, "HELL'S BELLS..." and the rope kept swinging more and more violently until I started getting a little scared myself. It seemed like the rope was trying to smash a stained glass window but it couldn't quite reach it. Then began a long chase scene which took me through the decaying industrial bowels of what I assume was the church basement.

Kevin Wahl, Student
Age: NA
Minneapolis, Minnesota

About six months ago, I had my first dream starring Bill Clinton. My fiancé and I were in the midst of final plans for our April 10, 1993, wedding. I began to have "purgatory" wedding dreams. In my dreams, nothing went according to plan. For example, my fiancé was wearing a dark brown leisure suit with high-water pants, I couldn't find my white pumps so I had to wear brown woven leather sandals, and we couldn't get into our church so the wedding ceremony was performed in an old barn, complete with straw and farm animals. But the one constant in all my dreams was Bill Clinton. In each dream, he was a guest at our wedding.

After having four of these dreams, I decided not to take any chances. Possibly, Bill Clinton was destined to be at our wedding. So we invited Bill and Hillary to our wedding. While they were unable to attend, they did send their regrets and best wishes on the official White House stationery.

Denise Drumm, Radiologic Technologist
Age: 29
Marshall, Michigan

I was very happy because the President was expected the next day and I was going to marry him. *With apologies to the First Lady—the apology was not part of the dream.*

Marian Wheeling, Retired
Age: 70
Kirkwood, Missouri

I received an invitation to my girlfriend Judy's wedding, to be held near Springfield, Illinois. For a wedding present, I somehow got President Clinton to attend the ceremony. Twelve Secret Service men—six on each side of the President—clamored into the wooden pew—in the middle of the church and *just* when

Judy was saying her vows. All the guests, of course, looked back and took snapshots of President Clinton and his Secret Service men. Bill tried to look tranquil as his Secret Service men fidgeted.

The President and his group then left abruptly (about four minutes after getting situated in the pew). The police escorting the President turned on their sirens full tilt as they sped down the country road. (Road dust filled the small white church—guests were choking.) I was very sorry about my whole idea, ruining Judy's wedding and spending tax money to boot.

Julia Anderson-Miller, Art Director for a Publishing House
Age: 36
Chicago, Illinois

Bill Clinton and I got married with just my sister there.

That night, I went into the bedroom, and my sister, fully clothed, was propped up at the foot of the bed, talking politics to Bill Clinton, propped up at the head, in his pajamas.

I hand-signaled my sister to get out of bed, but she just kept talking and motioning me to get in. So, since she refused to get out, I jumped in next to Bill.

He put his arms around me and kissed me on the lips and said, "I love you."

I said, "I think I love you, too." We were just laying there, while I was trying to think of a way to tell him that I had had a hysterectomy two weeks ago (which I had had), when about twenty people surrounded the bed and started talking politics.

M.H.S. (Female), Clerk in a Party Store
Age: 61
Farmington Hills, Michigan

what Will It Be, Bill?

My three brothers, President Clinton, and I were in my parents' dining room in West Point, Iowa. We were all playing Trivial Pursuit and drinking sixteen-ounce cans of Bud Light. Whenever someone landed on a yellow square, they could ask President Clinton a policy question.

After we finished several beers, I got up to get everyone refills. I asked President Clinton, "Bill, do you need anything?"

He responded, "I'll have a Muddy River."

"What's a Muddy River?" I asked.

President Clinton was astounded. He gibed, "You mean you grew up ten miles from the Mississippi and you don't know what a Muddy River is? Why, in Arkansas we drink them all the time."

"Well, I'd be glad to make you one; what's in it?" I asked.

Bill explained, "Half Bosnian coffee and half Asti Spumante."

I walked into my parents' kitchen, opened a cupboard, and found an open bottle of Asti Spumante. However, there was no Bosnian coffee. I shouted, "Bill, I found the Asti, but we're out of Bosnian coffee."

Joseph R. Fullenkamp, Attorney
Age: 29
South Bend, Indiana

Last night I had a dream about Bill. Bill and I are old friends. We stopped at the local bar called The Mood for a drink. He had a light beer and I had a C.C. and soda. He talked to the people about all the things he is trying to do.

I showed his men the way to the tollway to return to O'Hare Airport.

> Richard J. Hofstetter, Electrician
> Age: 60
> La Grange, Illinois

I'm an observer—at an outdoor party. A waitress asks the President if he'd like a drink. "Yes," he says. "A kangaroo, and make it orange."

> Wendy Vorce, Gardener at a Campground
> Age: 40
> Seaside, Oregon

world War II

I am on a flight across the country in a World War II biplane. I spend the night in Little Rock, and as I prepare for departure the following morning, I see a group of people jogging on the ramp at the airport when, suddenly, one person breaks away from the group. He heads towards my airplane and asks me if I can fly him to Hope, Arkansas. I am startled to see that it is the President!

I assure him that yes, I can drop him off at Hope, and he clambers aboard. As I introduce myself I tell him that I know where Hope is because I spent six weeks there during the summer of 1941. He exclaims that he wasn't even born yet in 1941, but goes on to tell me about the great watermelons grown there.

We fly to Hope, and after landing, he leaps out of the airplane and strides off in his jogging mode and is last seen heading away from the airport.

R.S.B., Captain, USN (Retired)
Age: 68
Mountain View, California

Its scenario was in Germany during the Battle of the Bulge. He (Clinton) is a visiting politico, and he is interviewing me in a machine gun nest, arduously scraped out of the frozen earth. As we talk, gunfire increases and grows nearer to us—suddenly out of a scrub of evergreens, a bunch of German infantry is running towards my position—I open fire and get them all, but as one falls into the snow he launches a signal flare. In a millisecond, I hear the clank of armor rolling towards us, and Clinton grabs my shoulder and says, "Hold fast, Smitty, I'll go for help," and off he goes. I never see him again in person, but having been overrun and taken prisoner, I do see him in a German mess as I drink beer with an SS Panzer sergeant. He is on TV (anachronism) and he is spinning a heroic tale to the press of how he fought with the machine gun of a fallen GI . . . and then, when out of ammo, escaped the oncoming German armor. He pays tribute to me and says the two of us "were great buddies." A lie, of course, since I had never seen him before that day. I curse and then wake up.

Rodger C. Smith, Purveyor of Nostalgia, Things Military
Age: 63
Pittsburgh, Pennsylvania

Not a Dream of Bill, But...

I dreamt that I was walking down a dusty farm road. Up ahead, I saw a lane leading to a small weather-beaten farmhouse. Much like Dorothy's home in Kansas. However, there was no farmyard activity about the place.

I carried a freshly baked apple pie in my hands as I rapped on the well-worn screen door. I remember knowing who would be there as Barbara Bush came to the door. I knew that they had lost the election and had been driven to this somewhat destitute exile. George Bush reluctantly approached and stood in his wife's shadow as I offered my "apple pie consolation."

Robert L. Maier, Chef
Age: NA
Holland, Ohio

If you have had a "Dream of Bill," and you would like to describe it for us, please write to:

Dreams of Bill
1340 W. Irving Park Road
Box 361
Chicago, IL 60613